# PAYROLL in 90 Minutes

The ideal approach to mastering a payroll system

## *Robert Leach*

2000

First published in 2006 by Management Books 2000 Ltd
Forge House, Limes Road
Kemble, Cirencester
Gloucestershire, GL7 6AD, UK
Tel:  0044 (0) 1285 771441
Fax: 0044 (0) 1285 771055
E-mail: info@mb2000.com
Web: www.mb2000.com

British Library Cataloguing in Publication Data is available

ISBN 1-85252-504-5

# Contents

# 1

## Introduction

### General

Payroll operates at the heart of any organisation. It is a vital but too often overlooked mainstay of every business which employs people. Particular issues for payroll are:

- one missed deadline can cause serious problems, as staff will not react well to not being paid on time
- it is no longer a simple accounting function, but a specialist and complex task
- the PAYE system is enforced with strict penalties
- many payroll provisions are rarely encountered
- payroll rules are constantly changing.

You will be able to read this guide in an hour and a half, although checking through all your payroll systems and making sure that each element of the operation is correct in terms of the relevant legislation and good organisational practice and will undoubtedly take you quite a bit longer.

# 2

# Setting Up a Payroll

## Authority

**Every employer must have a formal payroll procedure. One person is the payroll supervisor.**
The payroll supervisor must know from whom he can accept instructions about pay rises, notification of appointment and dismissal, and authorisation of holidays. There may be levels of authorisation. For example, a supervisor may authorise holidays while only a director may authorise dismissal. Whatever is established must be documented. All notifications given to the payroll department must be in writing, signed and dated. They must be filed.

## Number of payrolls

Normally an employer has just one payroll. However there are many circumstances where it can be convenient to have more than one.

- A separate payroll may be set up for directors and senior managers, where they do not wish their pay details to be known to payroll staff. This payroll may be operated by the payroll supervisor or a senior person in accounts.
- If the company pays pensions directly to ex-employees, it is advisable to have a separate pension payroll (see Pensions).
- If there is any group of employees whose pay circumstances are significantly different from others, it can be appropriate for them to be a separate payroll. Examples are employees who are paid on a different basis, at a different frequency (e.g. monthly rather than weekly), or who work overseas.

## Scope

The exact duties of the payroll department must be determined. These are always likely to include:

(a) calculating each employee's gross pay
(b) calculating statutory maternity pay and statutory sick pay
(c) calculating the tax and national insurance pay
(d) calculating each employee's net pay
(e) keeping records of pay, tax, national insurance etc
(f) preparing cash, cheques or bank forms to effect payment
(g) preparing monthly and annual returns for tax and NI purposes, and
(h) calculating totals of gross pay, tax etc for each payment run.

In addition, the payroll department may be required to:
(a) keep personnel records
(b) keep attendance records
(c) monitor holiday entitlement
(d) prepare statistics on payroll
(e) pay expenses
(f) operate the petty cash system
(g) prepare management accounts on the payroll.

## Integration of payroll

Payroll is often integrated with other parts of the employer's system, such as:
- time and attendance
- till reconciliation in retail
- human resources management.

## Payment methods

Wages are usually paid to employees in the form of:
- cash
- cheque
- bank transfer
- some other means.

Payments in **cash** have become less common, mainly because of the attendant high security and handling costs.

**Cheques** are simple to operate, though they generally require the employee to have a bank account. An employer cannot force an employee to open a bank account, though employees may be encouraged to do so by arrangement with a local bank. An employee without a bank account can still be paid by open cheque which can be cashed at the bank, or at another branch by special arrangement. From 1 January 2000, payment by **credit transfer** may only be done automatically. Credit transfers may only be made into bank or building society accounts, though most types of accounts can receive such funds. The payroll department must know the bank account details of all its employees.

**Automated credit transfer** can be done by using BACS operated by the clearing banks. Details on BACS are arranged through your bank. An alternative system of automated credit transfer is Giropay run by the Post Office.

## Confidentiality

Although payroll information is not automatically confidential under UK law, it is usual to treat it as such. This means that information about a particular employee should only be communicated to that employee or to another person authorised to see the information. Research has shown that employees are often more willing to confide in the payroll department than in other officers of the company.

As part of these arrangements, payroll records must be kept safe from accidental damage and unauthorised access.

## Accounting

Consideration must given on how much accounting information is to be extracted from the payroll function. Basic financial data, such as gross pay, PAYE totals etc will routinely be passed.

If management accounting is also required, this must be allowed for in setting up the payroll system at the outset.

## Accuracy

Payroll also has to work to particularly high standards of accuracy.

Paying too much creates problems of recovering the overpayment, while paying too little can result in payroll being required to run an additional payroll for the balance.

The matter of dealing with errors is covered in Chapter 3.

## Record-keeping

Payroll records must be kept for the three years before the current year, under PAYE rules. However, there are other rules which can require longer retention periods. In practice, it is usual to keep payroll records for the previous six years.

Whatever period is chosen, it is usually advisable to keep with them other payroll material, such as pay rates, company rules and tax tables for those years.

Payroll records may be kept in paper form in an archive, or may be kept on computer, microfilm, microfiche or optical disc. If stored other than paper, it is essential that the business either takes a paper print-out, or ensures that it keeps appropriate equipment and software for the discs or other media to be displayed. It should ensure that there are staff who remember how to use this equipment, and that any manuals are kept for it. Accessibility to archived records should always be considered when upgrading any computer or archiving system.

Once the time limit has expired, an employer may dispose of the payroll records. As payroll records can remain sensitive even many years later, it is advisable for the records to be burned or shredded rather than dumped.

## Payroll method

The employer must decide what method to use for operating the payroll. The choice is basically between:

- operating the payroll yourself, or
- using a bureau.

If operating the payroll yourself, the choice is usually between:

- a manual system, or
- a computer-based system.

A manual system may use a proprietary accounting system available from commercial stationers, or the forms provided free by HMRC.

For all but the smallest payrolls, a computer-based system is appropriate. If the payroll is straightforward, an 'off-the-shelf' package is sufficient. If the payroll system is not straightforward, you must check that the package can cope. A complicated payroll is one where:

- the method for calculating gross pay is complicated, or
- you have many types of deduction, or
- you require much analysis of payroll data.

The computer system has a master file of employee data, and transaction files for each payroll run. As payroll programs are no

*11*

longer written for each application but rather supplied as a ready-made package, it is not necessary for the payroll department to specify requirements. The software house provides details.

If using a bureau, you have a choice between:

- inputting the data yourself from a computer terminal, or
- supplying the data in manuscript or similar form and letting the bureau input it.

If the requirements are complex or unusual, the latter option is probably better. Any of the better bureaux is able to cope with whatever your requirements are. If they cannot cope with any requirement, find another bureau.

### Details on employees

It is not necessary for the payroll department to have copies of employees' contracts of employments. Indeed there may be good reasons why payroll should not see the contracts. However the payroll department must know sufficient details for each employee to run the payroll. These details include:

- the rate of pay
- frequency of payment
- method of payment
- period of notice
- whether the company may make payment in lieu of notice
- any provisions regarding overtime
- whether the employee is a member of any occupational scheme
- details of any occupational sick pay or occupational maternity pay
- any taxable benefits provided to employee, such as company car or beneficial loan
- details of eligibility for any profit-sharing or share option scheme
- employee's date of birth
- employee's gender
- employee's bank account details (if paying by credit transfer).

There must also be the facility to change any of these data, noting the date of the change and what they were before.

Depending on the scope of the payroll's duties, the department could also need to know:

- entitlement to holiday, including public holidays
- how holiday entitlement accrues
- how the final payslip is to be adjusted for holidays
- employee's address and telephone number

The employer's policy must also determine:
- a procedure for any employee who believes he has been wrongly paid
- any facilities for company loans or advances on salary.

It is usually necessary to have a system whereby an apparent breach of company policy can be referred for possible retrospective acceptance. For example, if an employee exceeds his holiday entitlement in one year, the management may be prepared to allow the employee to take the excess from a succeeding year's entitlement, even though this goes against company policy.

Any changes in these details must be notified to payroll with proper authority.

## Deadlines
Payroll has probably the strictest deadlines of any business function. The consequences of the payroll being one day late are far greater than if almost any other function is delayed.

Two series of deadlines must be compiled. The first relates to net pay, starting with the date on which payment is made to employees, and working back to the dates by which certain functions must be performed. The second series relates to statutory deadlines, mainly for submitting returns and paying PAYE.

## Timetable
Once the payroll system and methods have been established, it is necessary to produce a timetable of deadlines. The timetable should be regarded as an edict engraved in stone. The timetable is constructed by working backwards from pay day. This is usually an express term in contracts of employment.

Staff are almost always paid in arrears, but are usually entitled to have their pay by the last day of the week or month. For monthly paid staff, as the last day (except for February) can be the 30th on a Sunday, it is advisable to make payment no later than the 28th (26th in February) of the month.

Time needs to be allowed for cheques or credit transfers to clear. Cheques usually need three working days. This can mean that cheques may need to be prepared by 23rd of the month at the latest. BACS information is processed in 36 to 60 hours.

The payroll department needs time to prepare the input data and adjust the master files. This will depend entirely on the size of the workforce and the complexity of the pay system. From this a date is established, say the 13th of the month. This must be made known to managers and employees as the date beyond which any data submitted will not affect the next payroll run. If details of a pay rise or unpaid leave, for example, are received after this date, the adjustment will be made in the next payslip.

### Registering with HMRC
An employer or prospective employer must register with HM Revenue and Customs (HMRC).

Form P223 should be requested from the local tax office. This is a simple form asking some basic questions. Registration is now often made at the same time as registering for VAT. The employer is allocated a PAYE reference number.

### Data Protection Act
The Data Protection Act 1984 requires those who hold personal data on a computer to register and comply with certain requirements. From 1 March 2000, this is supplemented by Data Protection Act 1998.

Records which are kept purely to process a payroll do not need to be registered. However any additional information held on file brings the file within the scope of the Act. Thus a payroll can be brought within the scope of the Act by including telephone numbers, attendance records, disciplinary notes or references.

### Scope of personal details
The payroll department needs to know the following personal details of each employee:

- name – surname and first two forenames
- date of birth
- sex
- marital status (not strictly required, but useful to know)
- address (for sending documents in certain cases).

*14*

If an employee tells payroll that his or her name has changed, the payroll department must decide whether to accept the name change. Purported name changes can be used for fraud. Payroll is only obliged to accept a name change evidenced by a legal document or a letter from a doctor, priest, magistrate, solicitor or person of similar standing who knows the individual, confirming that the new name is being used for all purposes. Alternatively the person may swear an affidavit to that effect.

A person's sex is male or female as determined at birth. From 1 April 2005 a person may legally change his or her sex as evidenced by a Gender Recognition Certificate.

Marital status means: single, married, divorced, widowed, or (from 5 December 2005) in a civil partnership with someone of the same sex.

# 3

## Calculating Gross Pay

### Constituents

Gross pay is everything an employee is entitled to under his contract of employment.

Typically, gross pay comprises some of these elements for each employee:

- basic salary or wages
- overtime
- bonuses and commission
- most round sum allowances and similar payments
- the value of certain vouchers
- sick pay, including statutory sick pay;
- maternity pay, including statutory maternity pay
- holiday pay.

### National minimum wage

From 1 April 1999, it is a legal requirement that all workers are paid at least a national minimum wage. For most workers aged 22 and older, the national minimum wage is:

| From | Rate per hour |
| --- | --- |
| 1 October 2006 | £5.35 |
| 1 October 2005 | £5.05 |
| 1 October 2004 | £4.85 |

For workers aged between 18 and 21, the national minimum wage is:

| From | Rate per hour |
| --- | --- |
| 1 October 2006 | £4.45 |
| 1 October 2005 | £4.25 |
| 1 October 2004 | £4.10 |

For workers aged 16 or 17, the national minimum wage is £3.30 an hour (£3.00 before October 2006).

The following categories of worker are excluded from the national minimum wage:

- the genuinely self-employed
- workers under the age of 16
- apprentices aged 16 or in their first year of apprenticeship
- trainees on certain government funded schemes
- students on sandwich courses
- trainee teachers
- people living and working within a family household
- people who work on an informal arrangement, such as helping a neighbour with her shopping
- members of the armed forces
- prisoners
- voluntary workers
- workers outside the UK if they normally work outside the UK
- participants in a work rehabilitation scheme
- members of religious communities.

The national minimum wage must be paid for a pay reference period. This is normally the period covered by the payslip, typically a month or a week. The law does not require that the national minimum wage be paid for every hour worked, but that the total for the pay reference period exceeds the national minimum wage.

The national minimum wage applies to basic pay. This includes sales commissions and bonuses, but does not include overtime premiums, shift allowances, tips, rewards for good attendance, payments for being a first aid officer, and similar.

The national minimum wage only relates to payments in cash, with one exception for accommodation. Other benefits in kind, such as company cars and private health insurance, are ignored. Where accommodation is provided for an employee, this may be regarded as the equivalent of a payment of no more than £3.90 per calendar day (from 1 October 2005 to 30 September 2006 – the rate may change from 1 October 2006).

The national minimum wage must be paid for hours worked. All workers are classified into one of four categories as to how they are paid:

- time work, payment by the hour

- salaried-hours work, payment for doing a job over so many hours
- output work, paid entirely by results, such as a piece rate of so much per unit assembled
- unmeasured work, where there are no set hours.

For time work, working hours include hours when the worker is:
- at work and working
- at work and available for work, but is prevented from working
- being trained during normal working hours
- on call or on standby and is awake, not at home, and at or near the normal place of work.

For salaried-hours work, the main difference is that the national minimum wage must be paid for every hour for which the worker is entitled to be paid his normal wage. This means that sickness and lunch breaks will usually be included.

For output work, an employer may either ensure that the piece rate or commission is sufficient to cover the national minimum wage for hours actually worked, or may make a fair estimate agreement for the hours that the work should take. Such an agreement must be in writing, and must be fair.

Unmeasured work only applies when it is impossible to determine what hours the worker should work. It applies to a few people such as caretakers and domestic staff. The main provision is that it allows the employer and worker to come to a daily average agreement. This must be in writing and be realistic. It allows the national minimum wage to be paid for the hours agreed rather than the hours actually worked.

There are no specific records which must be kept to ensure compliance with the national minimum wage. Normal payroll records are usually sufficient. HMRC administers the national minimum wage and must be allowed access to the records to ensure compliance. Every worker has the right to inspect his own wage records to ensure compliance.

### Methods of calculating basic pay
The payroll department must have sufficient information to calculate every employee's gross pay. The method of doing this is likely to be:
- regular weekly or monthly wage
- hourly rate
- piece rate.

If paid weekly or monthly (or at some other defined regular interval), the payroll department simply needs to know the amount and frequency.

For an hourly rate, the payroll department must know for each payroll run:

- the number of hours worked
- the rules for paying those hours
- the rates for those hours.

There may be overtime rates payable at a premium. An employee has no legal right to work overtime, nor to be paid any overtime premium unless the contract of employment says so.

Piece rate applies when an employee is paid according to the amount of work done, such as units assembled. It is only appropriate when the employee is engaged on a task which can be readily measured, verified and recorded.

### Pro rata adjustments

Sometimes it is necessary to adjust the amount payable for gross pay. This commonly occurs for employees who are paid a fixed weekly or monthly rate but who are not entitled to a whole week's or month's pay. This commonly happens when the employee:

- starts or leaves during the week or month
- is engaged in industrial action
- takes unpaid leave.

The law is unclear on how salaries should be apportioned. Unless the contract of employment states otherwise, it is probably advisable that such adjustment be calculated on the basis of working days rather than calendar days. Thus if a person had two days' unpaid leave in a month with 21 working days, his gross pay would be reduced by 2/21.

### Bonuses and commissions

Bonuses and commissions which take the form of cash payment rather than gifts, are simply treated as additions to gross pay. They are subject to tax and national insurance.

The frequency of the commission must be defined, and the period to which it relates. For example, commission may be for sales in each calendar quarter payable at the end of the following month. So someone may earn commission from January to March which is paid on 30 April.

If commission is related to a figure which does not appear in the financial accounts, provision must be made for it to be available in time for the pay run. For example, if a salesman is to receive commission on his sales alone, the order entry system must be sufficient to ensure this information is readily determined and made available to payroll in time.

## Backpay

Backpay usually arises when a retrospective pay award is given. For example in August, a 5% pay rise may be agreed backdated to March. Such an award usually involves two separate payroll functions:

- an increase in the gross pay from the current month or week
- a one-off payment for previous months or weeks.

Details of a retrospective pay award must be expressed to payroll in clear and unambiguous terms. The employer must also decide whether to pay the backpay to employees who left between the backdate and agreement date.

The procedure for calculating backpay in outline is to determine for each employee:

- whether that employee has been continuously employed during the backpay period – if not, determine for how long the employee has been continuously engaged in this period
- whether the employee is entitled to pay for the whole period to the agreement date – an employee will not usually be entitled to backpay for periods of industrial action, maternity leave or unpaid holiday
- calculate the amount of backpay – it is essential that instructions to payroll are clear enough to know whether, for example, a percentage increase is to be applied to overtime and bonuses or just to the basic rate
- check whether any part of the backpay period falls within the eight-week 'relevant period' for calculating statutory maternity pay (the procedure of what to do if it does is explained in the chapter on statutory maternity pay).

Backpay is added to the gross pay for the pay period in which it is paid. It is simply treated as additional gross pay for that period, for all purposes.

No attempt must be made to recalculate the tax, national insurance or attachment of earnings orders for earlier pay periods.

Pay may be related to profits or performance. The tax benefits of profit-related pay were abolished in 2000.

## Grossing up

Occasionally, payroll needs to gross up a figure, such as in calculating the tax payable under a PAYE settlement agreement, the Taxed Award Scheme, or when the employer agrees to pay the employee's tax.

The formula for grossing up a percentage is:

$$G = \frac{100N}{100 - N}$$

where G is the grossed up percentage, and N is the net percentage.

For current and recent rates of tax, the grossed up rates are:

| Rate | Grossed-up rate |
|------|-----------------|
| 10%  | 11.11%          |
| 20%  | 25%             |
| 22%  | 28.21%          |
| 23%  | 29.87%          |
| 40%  | 66.67%          |
| 50%  | 100%            |

## Absence

Payroll's concern about absent employees is whether they are to be paid for that day's absence.

An employee has the legal right to be paid for reasonable time off work for:

- ante-natal visits
- certain activities as an official of a recognised trade union
- looking for alternative work while under notice of redundancy
- acting as a trustee of the employer's occupational pension fund
- acting as a safety representative
- help with rehabilitation, assessment or treatment of a disabled worker
- receiving appropriate education if the worker is under 18 and is of a low education.

In practice for most paid time off, no adjustment at all is needed for normal pay.

An employee has the legal right to time off, but no legal right to be paid by the employer for:

- jury service
- sitting as a magistrate
- working as a member of a local authority
- working as a member of a statutory tribunal
- working as a governor of a school or other educational establishment
- working as a member of a water authority or river pollution body
- working as a member of a board of visitors for a prison authority.

From 15 December 1999, an employee has the right to take unpaid leave to deal with an emergency involving an immediate family member or other dependant. This right is strictly regulated. The time taken off must be no more than necessary; the reason must be one of five specified in the Act (broadly death, injury, illness of any dependant, or a parent needing to attend a child's school).

From 15 December 1999, a separate right of parental leave is available in heavily restricted circumstances. This allows a parent up to 13 weeks' unpaid leave in respect of every child under the age of 5. Little use has been made of this right.

### Entitlement to holiday

All employees are entitled to four weeks' paid holiday by law. The contract of employment may allow additional holiday.

Bank holidays are not additional paid holidays (unless the contract of employment says so), but the government plans to change the law in 2006 to make them paid holidays.

Holiday pay is subject to tax and national insurance on the same basis as normal pay, even if paid in advance.

### Untaken holiday

When an employee leaves, it is normal to adjust the final figure for gross pay to allow for any untaken holiday leave. However, an employee is legally only entitled to a payment for:

- untaken statutory leave … and
- other untaken leave if the contract explicitly says so (unlikely).

## Industrial action

Industrial action is when an employee refuses to perform all or any of his duties of his employment. The main consequences of industrial action are that:

- the employee is not entitled to any payment for the period of the action
- no PAYE refunds may be paid during the period
- the period is excluded from reckonable service in determining employment rights.

An employee cannot be sacked during the first 13 weeks of any official action.

## Errors

A payroll system must be designed so that:

- errors are made as rare as possible
- errors can be promptly corrected
- an employee does not suffer unduly because of any payroll error.

Generally a mistake made on one payslip may be corrected on the next. However, this general rule has several exceptions. In some cases, an employer is prohibited by law from reclaiming an overpayment. There are also some circumstances which limit the tax or national insurance which may be reclaimed from the employee.

There is usually no great problem if an error amounts to an underpayment. The employer simply adds the amount underpaid to the next payslip.

If an employer overpays the gross pay, the employer may not always have the legal right to reclaim the overpayment. Whether an employer may reclaim an overpayment depends on whether the mistake arose from a matter of law or fact. The latter is more likely in practice.

If the mistake arose from a matter of law, an employer may only reclaim an overpayment if:

- the employee was aware of the mistake; and
- in all the circumstances, it would be inequitable for the employee to keep the overpayment.

If the mistake arose from a matter of fact, an employer may only reclaim an overpayment if:

- the employer had not led the employee to believe that the money was his

- the employee had not spent the money when the mistake was discovered
- the mistake was not primarily caused by the employee's error (such as a mistake in completing a timesheet).

## Tax and national insurance errors

Errors in tax and national insurance can usually be corrected in the same tax year. For national insurance, a correction must not result in more than double the correct amount of national insurance for that payslip. Any shortfall may be carried forward to a future payslip.

An employer may reclaim unpaid national insurance on a payslip up to the end of the current tax year or in the next tax year. Otherwise any under-deductions of tax or national insurance must be referred to HMRC.

# 4

# Net Pay Calculations

## Scope of deductions

Deductions from pay are limited to:
- (a) tax and national insurance
- (b) attachments of earnings order and similar
- (c) corrections of mistakes on previous payslips, when allowed
- (d) trade union dues authorised by employee
- (e) amounts which the employee has authorised in writing
- (f) amounts which are allowable under the contract of employment
- (g) deductions for shortfalls in the retail trade.

Items (a) and (b) are covered in separate chapters. The other items are explained below.

It should be noted that an employer cannot deduct money in other circumstances, however reasonable they may seem. For example, an employer cannot deduct from pay money which an employee has stolen, nor for goods supplied by the employer for which the employee has not paid. The employer must recover such money through court action. An employee who has an unauthorised deduction made from his pay, may go to an employment tribunal to have the deduction restored.

A complete non-payment of wages is regarded as the same as a 100% deduction, and entitles the employee to go to an employment tribunal.

## Trade union dues

It is common for trade union dues to be deducted from payslips and paid over to the trade union by the employer. This practice is generally known as 'check-off'. Such a scheme is entirely voluntary. From 23 June 1998, check-off payments are treated in the same way as any other deduction authorised by the employee. The main condition is simply that the employee authorised the deduction in writing before it was made.

## Amounts authorised by employee

An employee may voluntarily authorise the employer to make deductions from his pay. This may arise for:

- a specific payment – such as repayment of a loan, subscription to a social club, or payment for goods bought from the company; or
- payments that may arise under defined circumstances – such as an agreement to refund training expenses if the employee leaves before a stated date. In practice, there can be difficulties in enforcing such arrangements.

The authorisation must be signed before the event which gives rise to the deduction.

## Partnership shares

An employer may run an all-employee share plan (see chapter 12). Under this, the employee may have deductions made from his pay to buy partnership shares.

These deductions are made from gross pay. PAYE and national insurance is calculated on gross pay after the deduction has been made. This means that tax and NI relief is given at source.

## Amounts authorised under the contract of employment

An alternative means of authorising deductions is for the authorisation to be in the contract of employment itself. If the employee accepts the contract, he accepts that the deduction may be authorised.

## Deductions in the retail trade

A special category of deduction is made for employees in the retail trade regarding shortfalls of cash or stock.

The retail trade deduction provision is intended to cover the situation where it can be demonstrated that cash or goods have gone missing, but it is unclear how. It also covers such events as damaged stock, shoplifting, giving wrong change and accepting forged currency.

The employer may deduct from wages the cash or stock shortfall which arose while the employee was responsible for the cash or stock. The following conditions must be observed:

- the employment must be in the retail trade
- the employee must be notified in writing that such a claim is being made – this notice must be handed to the employee or posted to his last known address
- the loss must have arisen in the 12 months before the deduction is made.

The amount of deduction is limited to 10% of gross wages on any payslip, except the last one. Any amount in excess of the 10% may be carried forward to future payslips. On the last payslip given to an employee who is leaving, the whole amount of the deduction may be made, even if it exceeds 10% of gross wages. Note that, while the deduction is limited to 10% of gross wages, the deduction is made from net wages. The employee does not get tax or NI relief on a retail deduction.

It should be noted that these deductions are rarely made in practice, and are greatly resented when made.

## Payroll giving

Payroll giving is an arrangement whereby an employee may have an amount deducted from his gross pay to give to charity. It is sometimes known as Give As You Earn or GAYE.

By deducting the donation from gross pay, tax relief is given at source. There is no national insurance relief, so PAYE is calculated on gross pay after deduction, and national insurance on gross pay before deduction. The employer pays the money to a registered agency within 14 days. The agency must disburse the money to the charity nominated by the employee.

The scheme is completely voluntary. A charity is not obliged to register as an agency. An employer is not obliged to operate the system, and an employee is not obliged to participate.

From 6 April 2000, the upper limit for payroll giving is removed. The agency must pass the money to the nominated charity. If this is not possible, the money must be donated to a charity whose aims are similar. Between 1 April 2004 and 31 December 2006, HMRC provide some incentives to encourage small employers to use the scheme.

## Student loan recovery

From 6 April 2000, employers may be required to recover loans advanced to employees when they were students in further education. Student loan recovery only applies for students whose courses started after August 1998.

An employer only recovers loan if either he has received a start notice SL1, or the employee hands in a P45 with Y in the SL box. An employer must operate student loan recovery, even if the P45 relates to a previous tax year. An employer continues making deductions for student loan recovery until a stop notice SL2 is received.

HMRC administers the student loan recovery scheme but does not administer the student loans themselves. These are administered by the Students Loans Company. An employee who protests that he has never had a student loan, or has paid it off, must be referred to the Company. In the meantime, deductions must still be made.

The amount of the student loan recovery is 9% on the amount by which annual pay exceeds £15,000. So a student earning £20,000 a year is liable to repay 9% of £5,000, which is £450.

The figure of gross pay used is that on which class 1 national insurance is assessed. So it is before pension contributions and payroll giving, but after partnership shares.

There is no cumulation in student loan recovery. Each payslip is considered on its own. An employer must not try to recover loan from a previous payslip that was below the pro rata threshold.

If the employee has a council tax attachment of earnings order or community charge attachment of earnings order, no student loan recovery is made until these orders are fully paid. Similarly no student loan recovery is made for any payslip for which a Scottish arrestment of earnings applies.

## Tax credits

Between 2000 and 2005, the working family tax credit was usually paid through the payroll. This is being phased out as this book goes to press.

The tax credit has nothing to do with tax and is not a credit. It is a means-tested social security benefit, paid directly by the government.

# $\overline{\underline{5}}$
# PAYE (Pay As You Earn)

## Summary
There are three sets of routines for payroll:
- payroll runs
- monthly or quarterly PAYE returns
- annual PAYE returns.

For each routine, the employer should establish proper procedures and disciplines.

## Payroll runs
Payroll is paid weekly or monthly or at other intervals in 'runs'.

The basic steps in a payroll run can be summarised as:
- updating the records for employees who have joined or left since the previous payroll run
- updating the records of existing employees for such matters as changed tax and national insurance codes and changes in rates of pay
- for each employee obtaining from the appropriate management source any details of the employee such as unpaid time off, overtime, bonuses and commissions
- for each employee calculating any entitlement to one of the statutory payments (see below)
- determining any other elements of gross pay (e.g. luncheon vouchers, taxable round sum allowances etc)
- calculating any contributions to an occupational pension fund
- making any other adjustments from gross pay (e.g. payroll giving, correction of error on previous payslip)
- calculating income tax
- calculating national insurance
- determining net pay
- making any deductions from net pay (e.g. trade union dues, loan repayments, attachment of earnings orders)

- preparing cheques, bank transfer slips or other payment means
- producing payslips
- paying the employees.

The statutory payments are:
- statutory maternity pay (SMP)
- statutory sick pay (SSP)
- statutory adoption pay (SAP)
- statutory paternity pay (SPP).

### Adjusting tax codes
A tax code is determined from one of three sources:
- a valid P45 from a previous employer
- by following the P46 instructions for a new employee who does not have a P45
- from form P6(T) issued by HMRC to the employer adjusting an employee tax code.

Once a tax code has been determined for an employee, it will be adjusted by either:
- a blanket instruction, issued before the start of the tax year to which it relates, to increase all tax codes by so many points according to the final letter; or
- a revised form P6(T).

The form P6(T) just gives the tax code without any explanation of how it is determined.

### Adjusting NI letters
The national insurance code is determined according to the circumstances. In the absence of any instructions or evidence to the contrary an employee is assessed to national insurance under code A.

### Pension contributions
A pension scheme is usually administered separately from the payroll. The scheme will usually notify payroll of how much to deduct. This is usually expressed as a percentage of pensionable earnings. Note that 'pensionable earnings' will often not be the same as actual earnings. It is common for a pensionable earnings to be as at a certain date in the year. Subsequent pay rises do not become pensionable until the next date.

## PAYE payment: monthly or quarterly

The tax and national insurance collected by the employer is paid to the Collector of Taxes.

This may be paid quarterly if the employer believes that the average monthly amount payable does not exceed £1,500 a month.

Unless the employer makes quarterly payments, PAYE must be paid to the Collector monthly. HMRC provides a payment booklet P30BC and postage-paid envelopes to the Collector. The booklet contains tear-out payment slips similar to a bank paying-in book.

By 2009/10, all PAYE payments must be made electronically, with earlier start dates for businesses with 250 or more employees. Smaller businesses who file electronically earlier may claim incentive payments.

## PAYE: calculation

The PAYE payment slip only asks for two figures and their total. These are:

- income tax and
- national insurance.

Income tax is simply the tax deducted for the tax month or tax weeks in that tax month. Note that if you have paid holiday pay for a future tax week which falls in a future tax month, the tax for that week does not have to be included in the current payment. Any amounts paid as tax credits are deducted.

The figure for national insurance is the total of employer's and employees' national insurance less any deductions for statutory payments. Amounts recovered under the student loan recovery scheme are deducted.

Broadly, a deduction for statutory sick pay may only be made to the extent that the SSP paid for that tax month exceeds 13% of the employer's and employees' national insurance for the same month.

A deduction for the other three statutory payments may always be made for any month in which they have been paid. The amount which may be reclaimed is 104.5% if the employer qualifies for small employer's relief (see below), and 92% otherwise.

An employer qualifies for small employer's relief (SER) if the total of his employer's and employees' national insurance for the previous tax year did not exceed £20,000.

The deductions for statutory payments are made from the figure for employer's and employees' national insurance payable. If, unusually, this is insufficient, the excess may be deducted from the income tax payable. If, most unusually, this is also insufficient, the employer makes the return with no payment and asks for a refund.

### Year-end routines

At the end of the year, the payroll department must prepare the payslips for month 12 or quarter 4 in the normal way. However there are many additional tasks to complete. In particular, there are year-end deadlines with strict penalties. In addition there is a special procedure for weekly paid staff if there is a 53rd pay day in the tax year.

There are 52 weeks and 1 day in a tax year; 52 weeks and 2 days if the tax year ends in a leap year. Accordingly a weekly-paid employee who is paid on 5 April, or on 4 or 5 April in a leap year, will already have had his full 52 weeks' worth of tax allowance.

This final payslip of the year is known as 'week 53' for weekly paid employees, 'week 54' for fortnightly-paid employees, and 'week 56' for four-weekly paid employees.

The procedure for such extra weeks is to tax that one payslip using the employee's tax code on a 'week 1' basis.

National insurance is calculated on the normal weekly basis.

### PAYE year-end procedures

The PAYE year-end procedures may be broadly summed up as:
- the P35 annual statement and related forms
- the P14/P60 certificates for each employee
- the form P9D and P11D expense forms.

Some of these may now be filed electronically.

### Form P35

The form P35 is the annual PAYE return.

It has two sections. The first is a declaration mainly comprising tick boxes. This certifies that your submission is true and complete. The second is a list of all employees engaged during the tax year, including those who left during the year, detailing for each the income tax deducted, employee's national insurance deducted, and SSP and SMP paid.

The second section contains boxes in which these figures are totalled and other calculations made to arrive at the total income tax and national insurance due for the year.

### Form P14/P60

For each employee a P14/P60 form is completed. The P14 goes to HMRC; the P60 is given to each employee to tell them how much they have earned during the year and how much tax and national insurance has been deducted. The employee must keep this certificate in case any query arises on his tax. From 2003, an employer is allowed to issue a duplicate P60, but is not obliged to do so.

### Gross pay for tax purposes

Gross pay is the amount paid to the employee. Benefits in kind, such as a company car, are taxable, but are reported separately.

### Income tax codes understood

Income tax is calculated by reference to a tax code for each employee. This indicates the amount of 'adjustment pay' which must be used for each employee.

For codes comprising a number followed by the letter **L, P, T** or **V**, the number represents one tenth of the amount an employee is allowed to earn tax-free each year. So 450L means that the first £4,500 a year is tax free. The employee is allowed 1/52 of this amount each week or 1/12 each month.

For a code starting with **K** followed by a number, the number represents one tenth of the amount that must be added to calculate taxable pay. So a code of K200 means that the employer must add £2,000 to the person's gross pay to find taxable pay. This happens when someone receives many benefits in kind or has significant other income not taxed at source, such as a large pension.

Code **BR** means 'basic rate'. Tax is deducted at 22% of gross pay with no additions or deductions. It is commonly used for second jobs.

Code **NT** means 'no tax', where no tax is deducted. This can apply to foreign workers, where HMRC is satisfied that the person is really self-employed, or where other arrangements are made to collect tax.

Code **D0** is similar to BR, except that tax is deducted at 40% on all earnings.

### Dispensations

There are many benefits in kind which are both a taxable benefit and a deductible expense to the employee. This means that the employee should pay tax on the benefit and then claim back the tax.

To short-circuit this, it is possible for HMRC to give an employer a 'dispensation' when the employer provides such a benefit. This must first be agreed in writing with the tax inspector. The letter often imposes a maximum value of benefit per employee.

## PAYE settlement agreements

A PAYE settlement agreement (PSA) is an arrangement whereby an employer can pay the tax on certain benefits provided to employees. This is convenient when an employer provides a benefit to many employees, such as a big party. It is also used when an employer provides an award whose impact it does not want blunted with a tax bill.

A PSA may only cover a benefit which is:

● minor or
● irregularly incurred or
● impracticable to apportion between employees.

A PSA may not be used for any benefit paid in cash.

The value of a benefit provided must be grossed up by the employee's marginal rate of tax. So if the employee's highest tax rate is the basic rate of 22% and he is provided with £100 of minor benefit, tax of £28.21 is payable – 28.21% is the grossing up percentage for 22%.

The tax on a PSA is payable by 19 October immediately following the end of the tax year, but it should be noted that items to be included in a PSA must be agreed with the inspector by 6 July immediately following the end of the tax year.

Class 1B national insurance is payable on the tax paid under a PSA. It may also be payable on the value of the benefit itself.

# 6

# National Insurance Principles

## Introduction
National insurance is, strictly, not a tax at all but a compulsory insurance premium to pay for social security benefits. It is administered by HMRC.

There are six classes of national insurance. The most important is class 1, which is paid by both employer and employee.

An employer (but not the employee) also pays class 1A on the value of a car and its fuel, and class 1B on other employee benefits. Classes 2 and 4 are paid by the self-employed. Class 3 is a voluntary contribution payable by anyone who wants to make up their contribution record.

Contributions of classes 1, 2 and 3 go towards the person's contribution record which determines entitlement to some social security benefits, particularly the state retirement pension.

## Main points about class 1
The main points to note about class 1 contributions are:
- class 1 is paid on 'earnings'
- class 1 has two elements – a primary contribution paid by the employee, and a secondary contribution paid by the employer
- an employee only pays primary contributions between the ages of 16 and retirement age (65 for men, 60 for women until the year 2010)
- an employer pays secondary contributions for an employee aged 16 above. He does not stop paying contributions when the employee reaches retirement age
- there is an earnings threshold (£97 a week in 2006/07) below which neither employee nor employer pays national insurance
- there is a lower earnings limit (£84 a week for 2006/07) above which an employee is regarded as having paid national

insurance, even when none has been deducted
- there is an upper earnings limit (£645 a week for 2006/07). If an employee earns more than this limit, he pays just 1% national insurance on earnings above the limit. The employer pays national insurance on all earnings without limit
- the contribution rates of national insurance is reduced if the employee is in an occupational pension scheme
- some employees may be eligible to pay a reduced rate of national insurance, or not be liable at all.

### Earnings

Class 1 national insurance is payable on 'earnings' of an 'employed earner'. In practice, this applies to all employment income.

Whether someone is employed or not is determined by Inland Revenue according to criteria given in free leaflet IR56, explained in the chapter on Tax Principles.

In practice, national insurance and PAYE income tax are often charged on the same figure of gross pay. However, employers should realise that this is not always the case. For example, termination payments are subject to PAYE on amounts above £30,000, while exempt from national insurance regardless of amount. Other examples are provided in later chapters.

Benefits in kind, which are subject to PAYE under the P11D system (see section 9), may be subject to class 1A national insurance. When tax is paid under a PAYE settlement agreement (see section 5), class 1B national insurance may be payable. These are payable by the employer only, not the employee.

### Pensions payable

Pensions paid are not earnings, and are therefore not subject to class 1 national insurance. This applies even if the pension scheme is not approved, or the pensioner is below retirement age.

### Reduced rate

Up to 11 May 1977, a married woman could elect to pay a reduced rate of national insurance, currently 4.85%. For this, she has a reduced entitlement to social security benefits. This election is no longer available, but a married woman who had made the election may continue to exercise it provided the conditions are met. Once a woman has lost the right to pay these rights, she cannot resume the right.

A woman loses the right to continue an election to pay reduced rate national insurance if:

- she so decides and notifies the Contributions Agency
- her earnings are below the lower earnings limit for two consecutive tax years starting after 5 April 1978
- her marriage ends other than by the death of her husband
- she remarries ... or
- she accidentally pays or is credited with class 1 national insurance and does nothing to rectify the error.

A woman who is eligible is given a card CF383 which must be held by the employer while paying her at a reduced rate. If the woman has been in employment from before 1980, she may have a form CF380 instead. This remains valid only for that employment. If the woman has more than one employment, she may obtain further cards from the Contributions Agency. The introduction of earnings thresholds means that many women may now be better off giving up their right to pay reduced rate.

## Non liability

An employee can be not liable for national insurance for three main reasons:

- the upper earnings limit has been reached in other employments
- the employee is above pensionable age or below 16
- the employee is personally not liable.

If an employee already has earnings up to or exceeding the upper earnings limit in other employments, the employee does not pay any more national insurance. The employee can obtain a card RD950 which the employer holds. An employer must not excuse an employee from paying employees' national insurance on these grounds unless the employer holds this card.

If an employee is above the state retirement age, the employee is not liable to pay national insurance, though the employer continues paying employer's national insurance. The employee can produce card CF384 to confirm this, which the employer must hold. However an employer may accept any evidence of the employee's age, such as a pension book, driving licence, passport or birth certificate. Details of such evidence should be noted on file.

Up to the year 2010, the state retirement age is 65 for men and 60 for women. Between the years 2010 and 2020, the state retirement age is gradually equalised to 65 for women. This only affects women born after 5 April 1950.

Employees aged under 16 are similarly excused paying national insurance, as are their employers. Again, any reasonable evidence of age will be accepted, but the date of the 16th birthday must be noted so that national insurance can be deducted.

Age exemptions refer to when the payslip is prepared, not to when the payment was earned. Thus a payslip prepared on 27 May for an employee whose 16th birthday was the day before pays national insurance on the whole amount, even though he was under 16 for most of the pay period.

There are a few circumstances when an employee may be exempt from national insurance for other reasons, most commonly because the person has recently come from overseas. Non-liability for reasons other than age or other employment is evidenced by card CA2700 which must be held by the employer.

### Basis of calculation: introduction

National insurance is calculated separately for the employer and employee, as explained below. The system for calculating employees' national insurance is amended for directors.

If an employee earns below the lower earnings limit, no national insurance is payable. If an employee earns above the earnings threshhold, national insurance is payable on earnings above this limit, until the upper earnings limit is reached. For 2006/07, these limits are £97 and £645 a week. This means that an employee earning £100 a week pays national insurance on the £3 by which his earnings exceed the earnings threshold limit. An employee earning £1,000 a week pays national insurance on the £548 which lie between the limits, known as 'band earnings'.

The employer pays no national insurance on wages below the earnings threshold. This is £97 a week for 2006/07. The employer pays national insurance on the amount by which earnings exceed the earnings threshold. For 2006/07, the rate of employer's national insurance is 12.8%. There is no upper limit for employer's national insurance.

If the employee is a member of a contracted-out occupational pension scheme, the rates of national insurance are reduced for both employer and employee. The contracted out rebate applies to all income above the lower earnings limit. However, the introduction of an earnings threshold above the lower earnings limit means that there is now a slice of income on which zero national insurance is payable. Therefore the rebate on this slice of income becomes a negative amount of deduction for both employer and employee. The employee's rebate is used to reduced the total national insurance payable by the employee, but only to reduce it to zero. Any unused balance of the employee's rebate is added to the employer's rebate.

The system of national insurance has changed significantly in recent years. A particularly significant change is the introduction of an earnings threshold at a different rate from the lower earnings limit.

## Making the calculation

The calculation of national insurance is usually done either by using a computer program which gives effect to the calculations above, or by using tables provided by the Contributions Agency.

If using contribution tables, ensure that you have the tables for the correct tax year. Unlike some tax tables, national insurance tables always change each year. The correct tax year is that in which the payment is made. A payslip for the period 1-7 April 2007 uses the tables for 2007/08, even though five of the seven days fall in the 2006/07 tax year.

Also ensure that you use the correct table as identified by a single letter. There are three books of tables:

- A, B and C (not contracted-out)
- D, E and C (contracted-out in COSRS)
- F, G and S (contracted-out in COMPS).

HMRC does not automatically send out books any more. Instead employers are provided with a CD containing the tables. They can also be accessed from the HMRC website. Printed books may ordered using the Employer's Orderline.

In addition to these letters, the Contributions Agency uses:

- X to denote non-liability and
- Y to denote class 1A national insurance.

The tables are produced in multiples of £1 for weekly pay, and £4 for monthly pay. You use the figures for the exact amount or the next lowest amount. So a weekly figure of £108.90 would use the figures for £108.

## Payment periods

National insurance is always paid for a 'payment period'. This is usually a week or month, or a multiple of weeks or months.

There are two tables for each letter, one for weekly pay and one for monthly pay. Where an employee is not paid each week or month but is paid in multiples of weeks, the appropriate table is used with the figures multiplied. For example, an employee paid every four weeks will have national insurance calculated by taking the figures from the weekly table and multiplying them by four.

If an employee is paid more frequently than once a week, such as daily, national insurance must be calculated on a cumulative basis during the week. If an employee is paid for an odd number of days which are not an exact multiple of weeks or months, the employee must be paid by calculating an equivalent daily rate.

If an employee receives a second payment in the same payment period, that second payment is regarded as an addition to the first payment. The total national insurance for that payment period is calculated as if the payments were made together.

If an employee receives payments according to two series of different lengths, the payment period is the shorter interval. Thus, if an employee is paid his basic salary weekly but receives commission monthly, the pay period remains the week. The commission is added to the basic pay in the week it is paid.

If any element of pay is made retrospectively, national insurance is calculated according to the pay period in which it is paid, not when it was earned.

## Multiple employment

If an employee has more than one employment with the same employer, the sums earned are added together and treated as one for national insurance purposes. This also applies if the employee has employment with employers who are associated, such as companies in the same group.

If an employee has employments with independent employers, each employment calculates national insurance independently. This means, for example, that the employee will receive twice the benefit of the nil band on earnings up to the lower earnings limit. No attempt is made by HMRC to collect any extra national insurance from the employee in such circumstances.

If an employee has multiple employments which put the total

earnings above the upper earnings limit, all whole amounts of pay above the upper earnings limit may be paid without employees' national insurance if the employee obtains the appropriate card from HMRC. An employee may reclaim from HMRC employees' national insurance paid above the upper earnings limit in other circumstances.

## Errors

If an employer makes an error in calculating the national insurance, this may be corrected on another payslip in the same or next tax year. However this must not be done so as to double the amount of employees' national insurance on a payslip. If the additional employees' national insurance exceeds this limit, the excess must be carried forward to future payslips.

## Class 1A national insurance

Class 1A contributions are paid by the employer on the taxable value of benefits in kind. The taxable value is calculated in exactly the same way as for income tax.

The amount is the rate used for employer's national insurance in the year that the benefit provided. Note that this is usually the rate for the tax year before the year in which the class 1A national insurance is paid.

Class 1A national insurance is generally not payable in respect of any benefit:

- exempt from income tax under a statutory provision, extra-statutory concession or dispensation
- for which class 1 national insurance has been paid
- which is covered by a PAYE settlement agreement
- provided to an employee earning less than £8,500 a year
- specifically exempted from class 1A, such as workplace nursery vouchers.

Class 1A national insurance is payable by 19 July immediately after the end of the tax year.

## Class 1B national insurance

Class 1B national insurance was introduced on 6 April 1999. It is paid by the employer on:

- the value of any benefit subject to national insurance and
- any tax paid under a PAYE settlement agreement, whether or not the underlying benefit is subject to national insurance.

*41*

Class 1B is not payable for any benefit on which class 1 or class 1A national insurance has been paid.

Class 1B national insurance is also payable on the amount of income tax paid under a PAYE settlement agreement. This element of class 1B is thus a tax on a tax. Class 1B is assessed on the whole amount of tax payable under a PAYE settlement agreement, regardless of whether the underlying benefits in kind were assessed to any class of national insurance.

The rate of class 1B is 12.8%. This is the same as the rate of employer's national insurance under class 1.

Class 1B is payable by the employer only, not the employee. It must be paid by 19 October following the tax year in which the benefit was provided or to which the PAYE settlement agreement relates.

## Overseas dimension

If a UK employee travels overseas as part of his work, he continues to be subject to national insurance.

An additional payments to an employee working overseas which do no more than cover any additional expense of being overseas is not subject to national insurance. If an employee works overseas for 60 or more days and the employer pays for the employee's husband or wife and any dependent children to visit, that payment is not subject to national insurance.

A payment from overseas for a worker in the UK is usually treated as UK earnings and subject to national insurance. However if there is any doubt on the matter, the employer should contact HMRC for advice.

Under European law, an employee is only required to pay national insurance or its equivalent in one EU state on any particular earnings. This is usually the state where the employee is working. If it appears that an employee may be paying national insurance to more than one state, HMRC should be asked to resolve the matter.

When a worker migrates between EU states, the normal practice is that the worker continues paying national insurance (or its equivalent) in the first state for one year, and then pays in the new state.

## Administration

National insurance is now administered by HMRC.

A key part of the national insurance system is the national

insurance number. This comprises two letters, six digits and a letter in the form LLNNNNNNL. The letter at the end is not the employee's contribution letter. The national insurance number should be quoted in all correspondence and forms to Inland Revenue about that employee. There is a tracing system to help employers find the national insurance number.

Payment of class 1 national insurance is made as part of the PAYE system. Class 1A national insurance may be paid with the year-end return or separately. Class 1B is paid separately.

From 6 April 1999 there is a formal appeals procedure for national insurance which closely models the procedure for income tax.

# 7

## Employee Joining

### Introduction

Every new employee should be initiated into the company's employment as part of the personnel arrangements. Certain arrangements should be included in this process for payroll purposes. These relate almost entirely to tax and national insurance.

For tax and national insurance purposes, a new payroll record must be created every time an employee starts work, even if that employee was employed by the same employer earlier in the tax year. The payroll record comprises a P11 deductions sheet provided free by HMRC, or an equivalent in manuscript or computerised form.

Basically a new employee should either produce parts 2 and 3 of a P45 tax certificate, or a P46 tax certificate should be completed. Production of a P45 may be part of the procedure for ensuring that a new employee is not an illegal immigrant.

Some employees may have other certificates to hand in, such as a card showing that the employee is exempt from national insurance or may pay the reduced rate.

### The P45 certificate

A new employee should be asked if he has a P45 certificate. This is prepared by a previous employer, or by the Department of Works and Pensions if the employee was previously unemployed. The employee should have parts 2 and 3 of what was originally a four-part form.

If the employee hands over a P45, the employer:

- checks boxes 6 and 7 to see that the same figures appear on parts 2 and 3
- completes boxes 8 to 13
- records details from P45 on to form P11 or equivalent
- sends part 3 to the tax office and keeps part 2.

The tax office has a procedure for marrying part 1 from the old employer with part 3 from the new employer. If there is any discrepancy, the matter may be treated as a possible fraud.

What happens next depends on what is written on the P45. If the form gives a tax code, this is by the new employer if the P45 was issued:

- in the same tax year or
- in the previous tax year and the employment starts before 24 May of the current tax year.

If the code consists of a number with no letter as a suffix, the employer adds a T suffix in his own records, but must not add it to the P45 itself.

If the P45 indicates that the tax code was operated on a week 1 or month 1 basis, that basis is continued by the new employer.

If the P45 was issued in a current year, shows a cumulative tax code, and gives figures for pay and tax from the previous employment, those figures are entered in the payroll records as pay and tax from previous employment.

If the P45 shows tax and pay figures from the previous tax year and is taken on after 24 May in the current tax year, the emergency tax code must be used instead.

If there is a Y in box 5, the new employer must make student loan deductions.

### Tax on first payslip

The cumulative tax code system in PAYE can result in unusual amounts of tax on the first payslip.

If an employee has not worked for a while before starting the present job, he could pay little tax or even receive a refund on the first payslip. This reflects the tax allowances which have not been utilised during the period of non-work. A tax refund may be paid without limit and without obtaining permission from HMRC. It is no longer necessary to obtain HMRC permission to refund tax on a first payslip.

If an employee was paid in the same tax week or tax month as he starts his new job, he will already have received the tax allowance for that week or month in his last payslip in his old job. For that reason, his tax may be particularly large on his first payslip.

In both cases, it is advisable to explain the position to the employee, so that he does not assume that his net pay on the first payslip will be his net pay on future payslips.

## If no P45 is produced

If for any reason, an employee does not produce a P45, a P46 must be prepared and sent to the tax office. This procedure applies even if the employee has a P45 which he refuses to hand over, such as when he does not want the new employer to know where he worked before. In such cases, the employer should ask the employee to send both parts of the P45 to the tax office, and explain that the employee may be paying too much tax for a while. A form P46 must still be prepared.

The P46 is an A4-size two-part document, the top copy of which has a tear-off slip. There are three statements on the form marked A, B and C. The employee should tick which statement applies to him.

## The statements are:

**Statement A**
This is my first job since last 6 April and I have not been receiving taxable jobseeker's allowance or taxable incapacity benefit or a state or occupational pension.

**Statement B**
This is now my only job, but since last 6 April I have had another job, or have received taxable jobseeker's allowance or incapacity benefit. I do not receive a state or occupational pension.

**Statement C**
I have another job or receive a state or occupational pension.

**Student Loans**
If you left a course of Higher Education before last 6 April and received your first Student Loan instalment on or after 1 September 1998 and you have not fully repaid your student loan, tick box D. (If you are required to repay your student loan through your bank or building society do not tick box D.)

From 6 April 2006, only one box out of A, B and C may be ticked. Box D may be ticked in addition.

The tax code to be operated depends on which box is ticked, thus:

| Box ticked | Tax code |
|---|---|
| A | emergency code on a cumulative basis |
| B | emergency code on a week 1/month 1 basis |
| C | BR |

If an employee produces a P45 after the P46 procedure has been used, and the P45 is still valid, the employer may change the tax code to that shown on the P45, but operating the tax code on a week 1 or month 1 basis.

## National insurance number tracing

If a new employee does not give a national insurance number, a national insurance number trace form may be used. The form CA6855 is available free from Inland Revenue.

A form CA6856 giving the national insurance number is normally sent to the employer within a week giving the number. The number should be noted in the payroll records, and then this form passed to the employee. If a number cannot be traced, the employer will be advised of this.

## Emergency tax

Emergency tax is a temporary tax code which is used while an employee's proper tax code is being determined. It is always wrong as a permanent tax code.

The code for emergency tax code is announced each year by Inland Revenue in the PAYE literature. In practice, it is the main personal allowance with the final '5' replaced by 'L'. In 2006/07 this allowance is £5,035, so emergency tax is 503L. Emergency tax may be operated either on a cumulative basis, or a week 1/month 1 basis.

## National insurance

A new employee will often not bring any documents at all affecting his or her national insurance. In such cases, the employee will be allocated contribution letter D if in a contracted-out occupational pension scheme, or letter A if in a contracted-out scheme.

If an employee does provide certain documentation, a different contribution letter may be used, as noted below.

A certificate of non-liability is a card or form from the DWP numbered RD950, CF384 or CA2700, which are issued for different reasons of non-liability. Also an employee who is under 16, or over

60 (women) or 65 (men) is not liable to national insurance. Such an employee may also be regarded as not liable on production of proof of age (such as a driving licence, passport or birth certificate). For such employees, you use the contribution letter:
- S, if the employee is a COMPS member or
- C, if the employee is not.

Even though the employee is not liable to pay national insurance, the employer remains liable. Note that if you using table C or S because the employee is below 16, appropriate arrangements must be made to ensure that national insurance is operated from the week the employee becomes 16.

A woman may have a card CF383 or equivalent which indicates that she may pay reduced rate liability. The employer must check that the woman remains eligible to reduced rate contributions. For such an employee, you use the contribution letter:
- G, if the employee is a COMPS member
- E, if the employee is a member of an occupational pension scheme
- B, if the employee is a member of neither COMPS nor an occupational scheme.

For employees who produce no documentation at all, you use contribution letter:
- D, if the employee is a member of an occupational pension scheme or
- A, if not.

Contribution letter A is by far the commonest contribution letter used.

If a contribution letter depends on an employee producing a card from Inland Revenue, the employer must retain possession of the card while operating the appropriate contribution letter. If an employee needs two or more cards (such as if the employee has two or more jobs), the employee may be able to obtain further copies from HMRC – this is not the responsibility of the employer. The card must be returned to the employee when the employee leaves.

### Statutory sick pay
An employer is not required to ask a new employee if he has a form SSP1(L) from a previous employer. This form states that the

employee received statutory sick pay in the last eight weeks of the old employment. Its use is now voluntary at the employee's discretion. Further details are given in chapter 19 on Statutory Sick Pay.

## Foreign employees

Most foreign employees need a work permit to work in the UK. This does not apply to citizens of any state in the European Union. There are other exceptions.

The employer must check to see if it appears that the employee may work in the UK. It is sufficient for an employer to see a P45, P60 or payslip which appears to relate to the job applicant and has a valid national insurance number. Note that this does not mean that the employee may legally work in the UK; it simply prevents the employer being liable for a penalty under the Act.

Normal PAYE must be operated for:

- any employee working at the UK branch or office of an overseas business
- any employee working under the day-to-day control of a UK business or a UK branch of a foreign business.

## Employee going overseas

If an employee goes overseas for a short period, tax and national insurance is operated normally.

For longer periods, income tax remains payable in the normal way. If an employee is subject to foreign tax in addition to UK tax, the employee may claim double taxation relief.

# 8

# Employee Leaving

## Introduction

An employment may end in many ways, voluntary or involuntary, or a combination of both. If an employer makes a payment in respect of an employee leaving, such payment may be taxable as a termination payment.

## Payment

The employee is entitled to his full pay up to the last day. Sometimes employees who have been dismissed believe they are not entitled to their final pay. The full tax allowance for the tax week or month is used, even if the employee leaves before the end of it.

Care should be taken to see if the employee is entitled to any further payments. These may include ordinary pay if a 'cash in hand' system is being worked, or if the employee earns commission or bonuses. There may be an adjustment for holiday pay, though this is not usually a legal entitlement as explained in the chapter on Holidays. There may be adjustments for retail deductions, loan repayments, or tax refunds withheld because of industry action.

Where an employee leaves part way through a pay period such as a monthly paid worker leaving on the 21st, the final pay must be calculated pro rata. There is conflicting legal precedent on whether this should be done on a calendar day or working day basis, with probably the working day basis being the preferred method. This means that the final payslip may be calculated as 15/22 of a month rather than 21/31.

## The P45

The employer must prepare a form P45. Part 1 of the form is sent to the employer's tax office. Parts 1A, 2 and 3 are given to the employee. The employee keeps part 1A and hands part 2 and 3 to the new employer or to the Benefits Agency if claiming jobseeker's allowance.

You must never issue a duplicate P45. If an employee asks for another P45, you should refuse and instead provide a letter stating what information was on the P45.

## Payments after P45 issued

Sometimes a payment may be made to an employee after the P45 has been issued. You must under no circumstances issue a further P45 or attempt to alter the P45 you have issued.

The final payment is made subject to the BR tax code. These amounts are added to the figures of gross pay and tax as disclosed on the P14 form (which will also show BR tax code.)

The employee should be issued with a letter stating:

- the date of the payment
- the amount of the payment
- the amount of tax deducted.

## Retirement

When an employee retires, a P45 is normally issued in the normal way but with the word PENSIONER written on the top.

Exceptionally, the pensioner will continue to be paid by the employer. For such cases form P160 must be completed. This is now a two-part form. Part 1 is sent to the tax office; part 2 is kept by the employee.

It is more common for pensioners to be paid on a special pension payroll. Details on this are given in chapter 20.

## Termination payments

A payment on termination of employment may be tax-free under a specific provision, failing which it may come within the £30,000 limit for termination payments generally.

It is essential that the exact nature of the termination payment be established. It does not matter what the parties choose to call the payment, its purpose and legal basis must be established.

The following payments at the end of an employment are tax-free regardless of amount:

- statutory redundancy pay
- an ex gratia payment to an employee who has died or become disabled
- an ex gratia payment to someone with sufficient overseas service

- a lump sum from a pension fund and
- compensation for wrongful dismissal.

Any benefit which arises from the contract of employment is fully taxed regardless of amount.

Other termination payments are generally tax-free up to £30,000 per employee, above which they are fully taxed as income. Although statutory redundancy pay is not taxable, it must be included to see if the £30,000 limit has been reached.

These categories can involve fine distinctions with serious consequences.

Some payments made to overseas workers may also be tax-free.

A lump sum paid from a pension fund is tax-free. An employee is not taxed when an employer pays a lump sum into a pension fund for the benefit of the employee, nor if the employer provides a lump sum to buy an annuity for the employee. If a pension fund provides a refund of contributions, this is taxed at a special rate of 20%.

Any other payment related to a pension may be taxable if part of an arrangement between employer and employee. Such a payment is taxed unless the prior agreement of Inland Revenue has been obtained that the payment is not taxable.

## Compensation for wrongful dismissal

Wrongful dismissal is when an employee is dismissed in the wrong manner, such as when he is not given notice or when a disciplinary procedure has not been followed. (This procedure may have become established by custom and practice.) Wrongful dismissal must be distinguished from unfair dismissal which is when the employee is dismissed for an unfair reason.

Wrongful dismissal is a breach of contract by the employer. As such, compensation for it cannot be earnings and is therefore tax-free.

## Payment in lieu of notice

A payment in lieu of notice is taxable if it arises from the contract of employment.

In practice, this often means that if the contract of employment says that an employee is entitled to payment in lieu of notice, it is taxable. If the contract of employment gives a period of notice but does not mention payment in lieu of notice, it is not taxable. This is because the contract does not give the employer any right to dismiss without notice, so the employer has committed a breach of contract. The House of Lords considered these matters in the leading case of Delaney v Staples [1992] 1 All ER 609. Although this was not a tax case, Inland Revenue follows its decision.

This held that there are four types of payment in lieu of notice:

- paying someone normally but not requiring them to attend for work (this is often called 'garden leave')
- where the contract of employment expressly allows the employer to make a payment in lieu of notice
- where the employer and employee agree a termination for leaving (this is often called a golden handshake) and
- where the employer unilaterally makes a payment in lieu of notice.

The first three are taxable as normal earnings. Only the fourth is tax-free.

There have been further cases on this point.

## Redundancy

An employee who is made redundant because of a diminution in the employer's work on which he is engaged may be entitled to statutory redundancy pay.

To receive this payment, the employee must meet the eligibility conditions, one of which is that the employee has at least two years' service. No statutory redundancy pay is payable if the employee is offered alternative employment.

The amount of the statutory redundancy pay is calculated as so many weeks' pay up to a statutory limit. The number of weeks' pay is determined according to the employees' age.

Statutory redundancy pay is free of income tax and national insurance. If it is part of a termination payment, statutory redundancy pay must be included to see if the £30,000 limit has been reached.

Redundancy is itself a fair reason for dismissal, but an employee may still bring a claim that redundancy is not the real reason or that his selection for redundancy was unfair.

For the purposes of statutory redundancy pay, there must be a diminution in the work for the employee to do. Thus no longer needing an employee because of automation or computerisation is not redundancy for the purposes of redundancy pay.

An employee is eligible for statutory redundancy pay if the

employee has at least two years' service and is under retirement age.

There is no statutory redundancy if an employee is offered suitable alternative employment by the same or an associated employer. This applies whether or not the employee accepts the offer.

## Amount of statutory redundancy pay

The amount of statutory redundancy pay is calculated as so many weeks' pay according to the number of whole years for which the employee has reckonable service and the employee's age in each of those years.

If the amount of pay varies, the average of the previous 12 weeks is used. All contractual elements of the pay are included, such as contracted overtime. The week's pay is subject to a statutory maximum, revised each year on 1 February. The rate from 1 February 2006 is £290.

The number of weeks' pay per year of service is based on the number of whole years in which the employee's age fell in the appropriate band, thus:

| | |
|---|---|
| 18 to 21: | ½ week |
| 22 to 40: | 1 week |
| 41 to retirement: | 1½ weeks (subject to restrictions for the final 90 weeks). |

Thus the absolute maximum which can be paid as statutory redundancy pay is:

20 years x 1 1/2 weeks x £290 = £8,700.

This amount is restricted if a person is made redundant in the 90 weeks before retirement.

## Death of employee

The affairs of a dead person are dealt with by a personal representative (PR). This is an executor if the person left a valid will, or by an administrator if not.

On notification of an employee's death, the payroll department should:

● make up the final payslip, usually pro rata to the date of death – this should include any outstanding sick pay, holiday pay, commission etc
● end any payment of statutory sick pay or statutory maternity pay

*54*

- calculate the value of any beneficial loan to the date of death – there is no tax on any loan outstanding after death, nor on any loan written off or released on death
- calculate the tax on the final payslip in the normal way using the current tax code to the end of the tax week or tax month in which the employee died
- pay any tax rebates withheld because the employee had been taking industrial action
- not deduct any national insurance from pay made up after the death
- prepare a P45, entering 'D' in the death box, and sending all four parts to the tax office
- notify personnel and any pensions department for them to take action.

Note that if the employer pays any amount above that legally required, such as paying the whole month's salary, the excess is a gift to the late employee's estate. As such it is not pay.

The employment consequences of an employee's death are:

- the employment ends – however obligations made between employer and employee can continue, for example, a loan from the employer remains repayable
- arrangements must be made to pass any employee's personal property on company premises to his estate, and to recover any employer's property such as a company car
- if the employee died at work, there are appropriate legal requirements to be followed
- if the employee was a party to proceedings before an industrial tribunal or court, those proceedings lapse unless the employee's personal representative decides to continue them
- if the employee was under notice for what proves to be an unfair dismissal, the date of death is substituted for the date of expiry of the notice.

The tax consequences of an employee's death are:

- a tax rebate may be claimable for the unused personal allowance – this is because a person is entitled to a whole year's allowance for the year of death, but the PAYE system will only have allowed part of the allowance
- if the husband or wife was claiming the age allowance on the

basis of the partner's age, that allowance is lost from the start of the next tax year.

The national insurance consequences of death are:
- the employee pays no national insurance on payslips made up after death, even if it covers periods before death.
- a wife who was paying reduced rate contributions becomes liable to pay the full rate.

The pensions consequences of an employee's death depend on the terms of the scheme. It is likely to include the payment of a lump sum as death in service benefit (which is tax-free). It may also pay a pension to surviving dependents, or a pension guarantee if there are no surviving dependents.

# 9

# Expenses and Benefits

## Introduction

An employee may be provided with substantial benefits other than cash payments of pay. These benefits can give rise to a potential tax liability and, in some cases, a national insurance liability also. The employer must report benefits provided.

An employee is entitled to claim certain expenses against his income arising from his employment.

If these two simple principles were applied with no further provision, most employees would be required to supply long lists of non-cash benefits each year with a shorter list of tax-deductible expenses.

To avoid this, many special provisions have been introduced, namely:

- some benefits are excluded from tax completely
- where a benefit matches an expense, a dispensation may be granted
- an employer may pay the tax under a PAYE settlement agreement and
- an approximation may be used to value some benefits.

These provisions have led to a complex system. Indeed many of the problems incurred by payroll departments now relate to the correct treatment of tax and national insurance. The treatment of specific items of benefit are covered in their own chapters. This chapter explains the underlying principles, and the procedures which have been developed to give effect to those principles.

## Income tax on benefits

If a benefit is taxable, its value is calculated as the cost to the employer of providing the benefit, unless there is a specific provision to the contrary.

These general provisions are subject to a vast number of exceptions.

## Income tax and expenses

An employee may deduct from his income assessable as employment income (formerly Schedule E) an amount which the employee 'is obliged to incur and defray out of the emoluments of that office or employment' if this is expended 'wholly, exclusively and necessarily in the performance of the duties of the office or employment'.

These words provide seven conditions which an expense must meet to be tax deductible:

(1) the employee must be **obliged** to incur the expense
(2) the employee must **incur** the expense
(3) it must be **incurred from pay**
(4) it must be **wholly** for the employment
(5) it must be **exclusively** for the employment
(6) it must be **necessarily** for the employment and
(7) it must be incurred **in the performance** of the duties of employment.

If any condition is not met, the expense is not tax-deductible. For example, commuting to work is not incurred in the performance of the duties of employment but to get the employee to work to start performing those duties. Therefore normal commuting expenses fail the test in (7) and are not allowable.

## Tax-free benefits

Many benefits are specifically excluded from a tax charge by statute, concession or practice. Many of these areas are notoriously grey. Grey areas often involve when a benefit derives indirectly from employment.

Benefits exempted by law include:

- benefits from approved share schemes
- pension contributions
- living accommodation in certain circumstances
- car parking near work
- canteen facilities
- medical treatment outside the UK
- certain entertainment provided by a third party
- workplace nurseries

- mobile telephones
- personal loans up to £5,000
- adaptations to a company car for a disabled employee
- relocation expenses to £8,000
- travel by works bus
- sporting and recreational facilities provided by employer
- personal incidental expenses (PIEs) when away on work to £5 a day in UK or £10 overseas
- payment of subscription to professional body or learned society
- settling or insuring a liability arising from employment
- training for a new job
- outplacement counselling
- flat rate allowances for tools and special clothing
- luncheon vouchers to 15p a day
- directors' travel between group companies
- certain long service awards
- suggestion scheme awards (to various limits)
- travel when public transport is disrupted
- disabled employees travelling between home and work
- certain external training courses
- travel from the mainland to offshore oilrigs
- occasional late night journeys home from work
- small gifts from third parties to £150 per employee
- Christmas parties and similar functions to £150 per employee
- legal costs in settling a wrongful dismissal case
- costs in acquiring an asset from an employee
- certain meals for lorry drivers
- payments towards pension when employment terminated
- periodic medical check-ups
- employee's food and drink while entertaining customers
- any benefit worth less than £1 per employee per year.

Most exemptions are subject to their own rules and conditions.

## P11D and non-P11D employees

The taxation of benefits depends on whether the employee is within the scope of the P11D tax form. Such an employee is broadly one who either:

- earns £8,500 a year or more or
- is a director.

In determining whether the employee has earned £8,500 or more, the benefits must be valued on a P11D basis.

A non-P11D employee avoids tax completely on most benefits in kind. Such an employee pays no tax on the value of a company car, beneficial loan, accommodation. Such an employee is only liable to pay tax on these benefits:

- vouchers and credit cards
- amounts paid on behalf of employee (such as settlement of home telephone bill)
- goods supplied which could easily be sold
- relocation expenses above the £8,000 limit (see Chapter 15).

Such benefits for a non-P11D employee are generally disclosed on a form P9D. Benefits for other employees are generally disclosed on form P11D.

There is a further exception that if clothing is taxable, a P11D employee is assessed on the cost to the employer while an employee is assessed on the estimated second-hand value. This curious provision is a relic of the pre-1978 system of taxing benefits.

### Collecting tax on benefits

Tax on benefits is usually disclosed on the form P11D submitted for each applicable employee at the end of the tax year. There are three exceptions to this general rule:

- if the benefit is also a tax-deductible expense in the hands of the employee, it may be the subject of a dispensation
- if the benefit is not a tax-deductible expense, but is minor, irregularly provided or impracticable to apportion between employees, it may be taxed under a PAYE settlement agreement
- benefits which are close to cash, such as vouchers or gold or marketable securities, are added to gross pay and taxed under PAYE.

Other benefits are disclosed on form P11D, stating their value. The tax on them is usually collected by adjusting the employee's tax code.

### Valuation of benefits

The general rule for valuing benefits for a P11D employee is that the cost is the charge to the employer, not the benefit to the employee.

In most cases the value of the benefit is simply what the employer paid for it. The value must also include any related charges such as delivery and installation. It must also include VAT, even if the employer is able to reclaim this as input tax.

There are exceptions for many benefits for which special valuation provisions exist:

- company cars are assessed as a percentage of their list price
- car fuel benefits are assessed according to annual tables
- the use of assets is assessed at 20% of their value
- vans are assessed at a fixed amount
- beneficial loans are assessed by using an official rate of interest.

HMRC may agree approximations with the employer for other expenses where an exact value cannot be easily determined.

### Valuation of expenses

Where an expense is tax-deductible in the hands of an employee, the amount of the expense allowable is usually the amount the employee has paid. This includes related expenditure such as delivery, installation and VAT.

There are exceptions for:

- use of own car, for which special rates may be used
- tools and clothing for certain manual occupations, for which a flat rate agreed with the relevant trade union and given in concession A1 may be claimed.

In both these cases, the employee may claim his actual expenditure if he wishes.

# 10

## Company Cars

### Introduction
When an employer provides a company car to an employee, there are two tax implications:
- the employee pays more income tax and
- the employer pays additional national insurance.

These are calculated by reference to the list price of the car.

If the employer also provides petrol or diesel for the company car, there are three further tax implications:
- the employee pays even more income tax
- the employer pays even more national insurance and
- the employer may have to adjust his VAT returns.

These are calculated by reference to tables.

It should be appreciated that company cars have long ceased to be always tax-efficient. Since 1987, the government has sharply increased the tax charge for company cars and fuel. The present government announced in its 1998 Budget that the fuel charge would increase by 20% above inflation each year. If an employee makes little use of a company car, it is worth checking to see whether it may be more tax effective to pay him the additional salary, or to provide alternative benefits.

### Definition of company car
For these purposes, a car is a vehicle primarily designed to carry people rather than goods. Note that this definition is not the same as for other purposes. If a vehicle is designed primarily to carry goods, it is either a van or a goods vehicle, for which there are different tax provisions.

A company car is one which is available to an employee for private use. This may be in addition to any business use. Note that it is the availability which creates the tax charge. An employee remains liable for this tax charge if he chooses not to use the car for private use, or even if he is unable to use the car (such as by being in hospital or banned from driving).

A car is regarded as available to an employee if it is made available to any member of the employee's immediate family or household. So the tax charge cannot be avoided by providing the car to the employee's husband or wife.

If a company has cars which are not allocated to a specific employee but are available as needed, the cars are 'pool cars', not company cars. An employee who uses a pool car for business purposes and any incidental private use is not taxed for that use. Incidental private use commonly includes taking a car home to start a business journey from home next day, or visiting a theatre during a period away on business. An employee who uses a pool car for a private use, such as travelling to a doctor's appointment, is liable to a daily taxable benefit based on 1/365 of the amount payable if the car had been available for the whole year.

## Tax charge on car
The tax charge on the car is a percentage of its list price.

Up to 5 April 2001, the percentage was 35% which was reduced by one-third if the car was more than four years old at the end of the tax year.

The list price was also reduced if the number of business miles exceeds 2,500 in the tax year, and by two-thirds if the number of business miles exceeds 18,000 in the tax year.

From April 2002, the percentage is between 15% and 35% according to the amount of carbon dioxide contained in its exhaust. The age of the car and number of business miles become irrelevant. Exhaust emissions are available from the manufacturer. Figures for common makes of car are available on HMRC's website.

## List price
The list price is the original full price for the car when first sold. The price is not reduced by any discount which the employer was able to negotiate.

If a car was bought second-hand, the employer must find out what the original price was. If this is not known, the information can usually be obtained fairly easily from a motor dealer or the manufacturer. The employer must also know the value of any accessories fitted to the car.

The list price includes:
- (a) the full list price of the car
- (b) VAT (even if the employer is able to reclaim this as input tax)
- (c) delivery charges
- (d) normal number plates
- (e) car tax (which was abolished for cars supplied from 11 November 1992)
- (f) some adaptations for disabled drivers
- (g) most accessories fitted after the car was acquired.

The list price does not include:
- (a) running costs, such as petrol, insurance, breakdown cover and road tax
- (b) telephones
- (c) routine services, maintenance and repairs
- (d) the extra cost of obtaining personalised number plates
- (e) some accessories and
- (f) (from 6 April 1999) the cost of converting the car to gas fuel.

The list price is limited to £80,000. If an employee is provided with a more expensive car, the figure of £80,000 is used for list price.

For a classic car, the market value is substituted for the list price. For these purposes a classic car is any car over 15 years over with a market value over £15,000.

If the employee makes any contribution to the cost of the car, that cost is subtracted from the list price. The maximum subtraction is £5,000. Care should be taken with this provision as there have been some surprising decisions disallowing employee payments towards having a better car, and limiting the amount allowed when the employee insured the car.

If an employee is provided with two or more company cars, the extra cars are taxed at 35% of list price.

### Accessories

If the car is fitted with an accessory costing more than £100, this is usually added to the list price. The cost includes the fitting charge.

An accessory which was fitted before 1 August 1993 is not added to the list price, even if it cost more than £100.

Telephones in cars are not added to the list price, but are considered separately. Before 6 April 1999, the provision of a mobile telephone created a taxable benefit of £200. From 6 April 1999, this charge is abolished. This means that, from 6 April 1999, a mobile telephone provided in a car is not taxed at all.

The special provisions for adaptations for the disabled are explained below.

If an accessory is replaced by one of the same value, there is no adjustment to the list price.

If an accessory is replaced by a superior accessory, such as replacing a radio with a radio and CD player, the additional value of the accessory is added to the list price. However if an original item is replaced by a superior item, the whole cost of the superior item is added to the list price.

## Adaptations for the disabled

Certain adaptations for disabled people are excluded from the list price. For this exclusion to apply, the adaptation must meet one of two sets of conditions.

The first condition is that the adaptation is only of advantage to a disabled person. Examples of this include adaptations to accommodate a wheelchair, or any device to allow a car to be driven one-handed.

The alternative conditions are that the driver has a 'disabled' sign displayed and the adaptation is needed because of the disability. Thus power steering and automatic transmission are exempt for a badge-holder if they make the car easier for the badge-holder.

## Business miles

For the purpose of calculating business miles, a car is regarded as having travelled a mile if the car travelled under its own power. You ignore other mileage, such as on a ferry or being towed.

A business mile is basically one travelled in the course of the employer's business. This includes delivering goods, travelling to meet a customer or supplier, or collecting supplies.

Travel between home and work is not usually business mileage.

## Fuel

If the employer pays for the fuel which the employee uses for his private mileage, there are three further tax implications:

- the employee is assessed to tax on a notional figure for the fuel
- the employer pays class 1A national insurance and
- there may need to be a VAT adjustment.

### Income tax on fuel
From 6 April 2003, the fuel benefit is calculated as a percentage of a fixed figure. The percentage is the same as used to calculate the car benefit, and generally lies between 15% and 35%. The fixed figure has been £14,000 since the present system was introduced.

Before 6 April 2003, tables were used according to engine size.

### Class 1A national insurance
If an employer provides a company car for the employee's private use, the employer must pay an additional amount of national insurance known as class 1A.

This is paid by the employer only, not the employee. It is paid once a year by 19 July after the tax year to which it relates. So the class 1A national insurance for 2006/07 must be paid by 19 July 2007.

Class 1A national insurance is calculated by taking the figures used for income tax purposes for the company car and any fuel benefit, and multiplying it by the rate of employer's national insurance for the tax year in which the car was provided. This means that the rate paid by 19 July 2007 must use the employer's national insurance rate for 2006/07, not the rate for 2007/08. Using the wrong rate is a common mistake.

### Value added tax
An employer who pays for an employee's private fuel has a choice whether to claim back the VAT on the fuel. If the employer chooses not to do so, no adjustment is needed to the VAT return.

If the employer does choose to do so, an adjustment must be made to the VAT return. This adjustment is intended to reflect the notional sale of fuel by the employer to the employee by requiring an addition to be made to the input tax for the period covered by the return. The addition is calculated by reference to tables produced for the purpose. These tables are not the same as those used for income tax or class 1A national insurance.

### Vans
For the purposes of payroll, a van is a vehicle which weighs no more

than 3.5 tonnes and is primarily intended to carry goods rather than people. Note that tax law contains other definitions for other purposes.

If an employee uses for his personal use, an employer's vehicle other than a car or van, the employee is taxed on the use of the vehicle as an asset made available to him.

An employee who uses the employer's van for personal use is liable to a tax charge.

From 6 April 2007, the standard charge is £3,000 per van. Previously the figure was £500 per van, or £350 if the van was more than four years old at the end of the tax year.

# 11

# Travel and Subsistence

## Introduction

An employer may reimburse an employee for the costs of travelling and subsistence on business. Subsistence comprises mainly hotel accommodation and meals.

The first point to note is that any entitlement by an employee for such payments is purely a matter for negotiation between employer and employee. The detailed rules on what may be paid tax-free do not in themselves create any legal entitlement to payment. However, an employee who is not fully reimbursed for the cost of business travel and subsistence may be able to claim tax relief on the unreimbursed element.

For tax purposes, it is necessary to determine how much of those expenses are regarded as pay. This involves:

- determining how much the employee has been reimbursed
- whether the trip counts as business trip (failing which the whole amount is usually gross pay) and
- if so, how much may be allowed for determining how much is taxable.

It should be remembered that there was a major revision of the tax treatment of travelling expenses from April 1998.

## Business trip

For any element of expenditure to be allowable, the travel and subsistence must relate to a business trip. Commuting between home and work is not usually business travel.

The following are regarded as business travel, meaning that reimbursement is not regarded as pay:

- visits made for business purposes, such as seeing a customer or supplier
- transport home when public transport is disrupted

- transport home when an employee is required to work late occasionally (see below)
- travel overseas to work (usually)
- a director or other employee travelling between companies in the same group
- an oilrig worker travelling from the mainland to the rig
- travel from home to work by a disabled person who cannot reasonably use normal transport
- certain work-related travel by diplomats and politicians.

The concession for working late occasionally only applies if:
- the employee is not required to work late on a regular basis, such as every Friday
- the employee is not required to work late more than 60 times a year
- the journey starts after 9pm and
- by the time the employee leaves, public transport has stopped or becomes too unreliable to expect the employee to use it.

There are many other tax exemptions which can exempt travel. These include training, third party gifts, Christmas parties, and relocation.

There is no payroll implication if the travel is made in a company car as this is taxed separately.

There is a House of Lords case, Pook v Owen [1969] 2 All ER 1, in which a doctor on-call was able to claim for his travel from home to the hospital because he had started to give instructions by telephone before he left home. This was held to be sufficient to make his travel to the hospital 'in the course of' his duties. However this case has not been widely followed, and care should be taken in using this precedent.

## Triangular travel

Triangular travel is when an employee travels direct from home to a place other than his normal place of work. An example is when an employee leaves home and drives straight to see a customer.

Example – an employee normally drives 12 miles to work. One day he drives straight to a customer who is 10 miles from the office and 15 miles from his home.

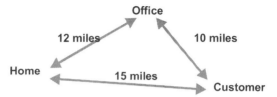

The employer may reimburse tax-free the lower of:
- the actual journey and
- the distance from the customer to the place of work.

Suppose the employer paid for the full return journey of 30 miles. As the return distance from work to the customer is only 20 miles, only that element of the payment is free of tax.

## Site working

An employee may work for more than one day at a site other than his normal place of work. The issue then becomes when the site becomes his normal place of work so that the provisions of triangular travel cease to apply.

A site is a temporary place of work, allowing some element of commuting there to be tax-free if:
- the employee is expected to work at the site for not more than 24 months and
- the employee does not work at the site for more than 24 months.

If it becomes clear during any of the above that the site work has lasted or is expected to last for more than 24 months, the site becomes the normal place of work from the day of change. No attempt should be made to adjust payments before the change.

## Working from home

An employee may be able to demonstrate that his normal place of work is his home. This will have the effect of making most travel related to work 'in the performance of' the duties of the work, and thus allow much more travel expense to be tax-free.

In practice it is difficult to establish that a person's home is his normal place of work. Any workplace provided by an employer is likely to prove fatal to such a claim. The fact that an employee chooses to work at home and the employer agrees is not sufficient to meet the 'necessary' test. Similarly, the fact that the employee is required to do some work at home is insufficient.

## Employee's own vehicle

An employee who uses his own vehicle for business may claim for the use of that vehicle. From 6 April 2002, a new system of flat rate mileage allowances was introduced for employees using their own transport for business journeys. It is not necessary to obtain a dispensation to use these rates.

If an employer and employee agree a lower rate of reimbursement, the employee may claim the shortfall as a tax deduction. If the employer and employee agree a higher rate, the excess is taxable as earnings. The treatment for national insurance is now the same as for income tax.

Currently (2006/07), the rate is 40p for the first 10,000 miles in any tax year, and 25p per mile thereafter, regardless of engine size.

The same rate may be used for business use of an employee's van.

A further 5p a mile is allowed if the employee carried a passenger.

For business use of an employee's motor cycle, a rate of 24p a mile may be used.

For business use of an employee's bicycle, an employer may use a rate of 20p a mile.

An employee is not entitled to demand such payment as of legal right; the amount of any reimbursement is always a matter for employer and employee to agree. If the employer pays a rate above these figures, the excess is taxed. If the employer pays less than these figures, the employee may claim the shortfall as tax relief.

The rates are also used for national insurance purposes, except that before 2001/02, there was no reduction in rate once 4,000 business miles had been travelled.

If an employee uses any other form of his transport on business (such as a boat or horse), the employer may agree a dispensation with Inland Revenue.

## Hotels

While away on business, an employee may claim for the cost of overnight accommodation and meals eaten away. A particularly extravagant hotel may have some element disallowed, though this rarely happens in practice.

An employee may be reimbursed tax-free the cost of three full meals a day, including alcoholic drink with the main meal. The employee may also be reimbursed tax-free for soft drinks between meals.

### Personal incidental expenses

An employee may also be reimbursed tax-free up to £5 a night (for stays in the UK) or £10 (overseas) for personal incidental expenses (PIEs). This is intended to cover miscellaneous small bits of hotel bills, such as personal telephone calls, newspapers, laundry, bar drinks etc.

The limit is applied per stay. So if an employee incurs PIEs of £10 on the first day in the UK, and £2 for each of the next four days, his total of £18 is within the £25 limit for five days. The figure must include VAT even if the employer is able to reclaim it.

The expenditure may be incurred in any way. The employee may have been given an advance, the employer may pay the bill directly, or the employer may reimburse the employee. This limit only applies to PIEs reimbursed by the employer. If an employer does not reimburse a PIE, the employee cannot use the limit to claim any tax relief. The measure was introduced to save payrollers having to comb hotel bills looking for disallowable expenditure to add to gross pay.

Where several employees stay in a hotel and it is not easy to establish exactly who incurred what PIE, Inland Revenue will accept any reasonable basis of apportionment.

If a PIE exceeds the limit, the whole amount of the PIE, not just the excess, is taxable unless the employee is obliged to pay for the excess himself. This requires:

- a company rule that the excess be repaid and
- repayment within a reasonable period (not defined).

The relief for PIEs does not need to be claimed by an employee, nor does it need a dispensation. Amounts of PIEs are not disclosed on form P9D or P11D.

# 12

# Share Schemes

## Introduction

Since 1978, the government has used the tax system to encourage employers to issue shares in itself to employees. This is based on research which indicates that productivity increases when an employee has an interest in his employer's profitability. Methods range from profit-sharing arrangements to schemes in which employees acquire shares (if the employer is a company).

It must be appreciated that once the employee legally owns the shares, he is usually in the same position as any other shareholder. He has the same rights to attend general meetings, ask questions and vote on resolutions.

If an employee gains shares free or at a special rate, this is a benefit in kind which arises from employment. Such shares are therefore taxable unless they come within the scope of some special exemptions. These exemptions relate almost entirely to avoiding the Schedule E (now called 'employment income') charge when the shares are issued. The employee usually remains liable to income tax on the dividends and to capital gains tax on any profit on disposal. In practice, this is unlikely to be a problem. Dividends are usually paid with the tax already deducted, and all but the largest capital gains will be covered by the annual exemption.

## Schemes

There are three types of option scheme. With their legislative source in Income and Corporation Taxes Act 1988, they are:

- company share option plans, previously known as executive share options, or just share options (s186);
- savings-related option schemes (s185(1)-(4)); and
- profit-sharing (s185(5)-(9)).

Profit-sharing schemes lose their special tax status for awards of shares made after 31 December 2002.

All these schemes must be registered with Inland Revenue. There are also special rules regarding:

- employee share option plans (ESOPs)
- preferential share purchase and
- unauthorised options.

In addition, from 2000, there are the enterprise management incentive (EMI) for senior employees and all-employee share plans for all employees. The latter is introduced by Finance Act 2000 s47 and Schedule 8.

It should be appreciated that most share schemes involve the issue of new shares to employees. As this amounts to a dilution of capital, the company must ensure that such issue is permitted under its articles of association.

### Company share option plans

This scheme was originally introduced in 1984 and was severely restricted from 17 July 1995. The main change was a reduction in the value of options which may be held under the scheme to £30,000. Previously it was the higher of £100,000 or four times salary. There is no tax liability when the option is grant nor when exercised.

The main conditions for a company share option plan are:

- the holder must not own more than 10% of the share capital
- there is a limit of £30,000 per employee. This is measured according to the share value on the day the option was granted
- the option must be to buy shares at whatever their value was when the option was granted
- the option must be exercised between three and ten years after being granted
- the option must be exercised no more frequently than once every three years
- the holder must have been a director or employee when the option was granted, but need not be when the option is exercised
- the shares must not be subject to any restriction other than a requirement to sell them when the employment ends
- the shares must be fully paid-up ordinary shares (except that a registered workers' co-operative may use redeemable shares) and

74

● the options must not be transferable.

## Savings-related option schemes

These schemes were first introduced in 1980. They allow employees to invest a monthly amount of up to £250 in share options for three, five or seven years. This amount is then used to buy shares in the employer at the option price.

Three-year contracts were introduced in April 1996. At the end of the term, a bonus is added equal to a multiple of the monthly payment. These multiples change about once a year or so. The latest figures (from 1 September 2005) are:

● 1.4 times for a three-year contract
● 4.4 times for a five-year contract
● 8.4 times for a seven-year contract.

A five-year contract repaid between the fifth and seventh anniversaries is worth 69 times the contribution plus interest at 3% from the fifth anniversary.

The main conditions are that:

● the holder does not own more than 25% of the share capital;
● the holder is not a part-time director (but a part-time employee may be included from 1 May 1995);
● the money invested is held in a Save As You Earn (SAYE) contract similar to those run by building societies;
● the scheme does not prescribe a maximum monthly contribution above £250;
● the scheme does not prescribe a minimum monthly contribution above £10 (though there are plans to reduce this to £5);
● the future share purchase is not less than 80% of the share's market value when the option is granted;
● the option cannot be exercised before the agreed expiry date (though there are exceptions for disability and redundancy).

## Employee share option plans (ESOPs)

An ESOP is a trust set up to acquire shares in the employer for the benefit of employees.

There is no tax advantage to an employee in an ESOP, but there is an advantage to the employer. Broadly the employer may claim relief for corporation tax for payments into an ESOP if certain conditions are met. There is also a provision whereby an ESOP may rollover capital gains.

## Profit-sharing

Profit-sharing allows an employer simply to give shares to an employee. This scheme was established in 1978, but lost its tax advantages from 2003.

The maximum amount which may be given to an employee is the greater of £3,000 and 10% of salary (to a maximum of £8,000).

Until the shares are sold, they are held in a trust. From 29 April 1996, there was no tax charge if the shares are sold after three years.

## Preferential share purchase

If the employer issues new shares, it is common for an employee to be able to participate on terms better than those available to other investors.

This benefit can have two elements:
● obtaining a higher allocation from the same subscription and
● buying shares at a lower price.

For tax purposes, only the latter is regarded as a benefit in kind, though the value is determined on the actual allocation.

For example, an employee applies for 500 shares at a special price of 90p each and is allocated 400. Another investor has to pay £1 each and would have only been allocated 300. The employee is liable to Schedule E tax on £40, the 10p saving on the 400 shares he was allocated.

## Unapproved plans

Until the 1996 Budget there was a measure of tax relief for share and option schemes which had not been approved by Inland Revenue. This was that an employee is liable to tax on the value of shares in the employer provided by the employer. Shares in other companies and other forms of security had already been made subject to tax and national insurance.

Now all shares provided to an employee are subject to tax and national insurance unless part of an Inland Revenue scheme. However there is a provision allowing for the tax to be paid in instalments.

## Enterprise management incentive

Independent trading companies with gross assets not exceeding £30 million will be able to award key employees (prior to 5 April 2001, limited to 15 key employees) with tax advantaged share options, each receiving options worth up to £100,000 at the time of grant.

There is no tax charge on the grant of the option and there will be normally no tax or National Insurance for the employee to pay when the options are exercised; nor will there normally be any National Insurance charge for the employer.

From 15 May 2000, the 15 employee limit was replaced by a limit of £3 million on the total value of the shares for which there are unexercised share options. Also, the scheme is no longer limited to key employees.

## All-employee share plan

From 28 July 2000, a company may operate an all-employee share plan (AESOP) to provide shares to employees. The shares are held in a trust for the employees. If held in the trust for at least five years, the employee pays no tax on this benefit.

An AESOP must be approved by Inland Revenue. It is subject to many conditions. In general, an AESOP must be open to all employees on equal terms, except that the entitlement to free shares (explained below) may be limited to remuneration, length of service or hours worked. Free shares may also be made conditional on reaching performance targets.

There are four types of share issue under an AESOP, though it should be noted that the shares themselves are of the same type under each issue:

- free shares
- partnership shares
- matching shares
- dividend shares.

Free shares are issued by the employer at no charge to the employee for whose benefit they are held. Up to £3,000 per employee per year may be issued.

Partnership shares are bought by the employee. Up to £1,500 may be bought by each employee each year. The amount must be collected through the payroll. It is deducted from gross pay before PAYE and national insurance are deducted. PAYE and national insurance are calculated on the net amount. This means that tax and national insurance relief is given at source on these shares.

Matching shares are further free shares which an employer may issue in a predetermined ratio to partnership shares. Up to £3,000 worth of matching shares may be issued per employee per year.

Dividends on the shares may either be paid to the employees (with tax deducted as for any other dividend), or it may be reinvested tax-free by buying dividend shares.

# 13

# Accommodation

## Introduction

If an employer provides living accommodation for an employee, there may be a tax liability on the employee for the benefit in kind. The provisions regarding temporary accommodation, such as hotels on business trips, are explained in the chapter on travelling expenses. Accommodation can in some cases count towards the national minimum wage.

A tax liability can have several separate elements:

(a) a general charge for the provision of living accommodation (with exceptions)
(b) an additional charge if the accommodation is expensive
(c) a charge on accommodation expenses borne by the employer
(d) a charge on relocation expenses above a limit.

Generally, the employer will declare these items of expenditure on a P11D form at the end of the year. HMRC will usually collect the tax by adjusting the employee's tax code. Amounts subject to tax under (c) and (d) above may be collected by a PAYE settlement agreement (see separate chapter).

## General charge on living accommodation

There is a tax charge if an employer provides living accommodation to an employee except when:

- the employee lives in the property to perform the duties properly (such as for a hospital doctor or hotel porter)
- the employment involves a special risk, and the accommodation is provided for the employee's safety (such as when the work makes the employee a target of a terrorist organisation)
- it is customary in that type of employment for the work to have property provided and such provision helps the

employee to do the job better (such as caretakers and vicars)
- the accommodation is free board and lodging for agricultural workers or
- the employee only uses that accommodation while away on his employer's business.

The employee is assessed to tax on the rateable value of the property. This is the notional amount payable if the property was rented. It was used to calculate 'the rates'. The rates were abolished in Scotland in 1989, and in England and Wales in 1990 when they were replaced by the community charge, now replaced by the council tax. Accordingly, the value must now be agreed with the valuer's office. This does not apply in Northern Ireland, where the rates are still applied.

If the employee pays an amount in respect of rent, that amount is deducted from the notional benefit to calculate his taxable benefit.

### Expensive accommodation

If the accommodation is 'expensive', there is an additional charge.

Accommodation is expensive if cost more than £75,000 when bought. If the house was bought more than six years before the employee occupied it, it is expensive if it was worth more than £75,000 when first occupied by the employee. The £75,000 limit has remained unchanged since 1983.

The charge is the excess above £75,000 multiplied by the official rate of interest, which is also used to calculate the tax of a beneficial loan.

If an employee is assessed on the open market rental value of the property, this additional tax charge is not made.

### Accommodation expenses

Generally, an employee is also assessed to tax on any accommodation expenses borne by the employer. These include heating, lighting, insurance, maintenance, water, cleaning and similar charges.

Furniture provided is generally taxed on the same basis as assets provided to an employer, basically an annual charge of 20% of the assets' value. However, for furniture, this charge is limited to 10% of the employee's net emoluments. 'Net emoluments' for these purposes are total income including taxable fringe benefits (except this furniture charge itself) less pension contributions and expense claims.

The tax charge for accommodation expenses applies whether or not the accommodation belongs to the employee. If the accommodation belongs to the employer, the charge for accommodation expenses may be additional to the other tax charges mentioned above.

If the employer pays any part of an employee's council tax (whether or not the employer owns the property), the employee is regarded as having received a taxable benefit. However if some of the accommodation is used for the employer's business, the employee may be able to claim a proportion as an employment (old Schedule E) expense. The rules were different for community charge (poll tax) and the rates.

Similarly, elements of other household expenses may be treated as an employment expense. A common example is the home telephone bill, a proportion of which may be regarded as for the employer's business. In practice, an employer can obtain a dispensation allowing for some telephone expenses to be paid without having to deduct tax or declare the payment on a form P11D. Any tax may be paid under a PAYE settlement agreement.

If the employer pays an accommodation expense which is the personal liability of an employee, there is also a national insurance liability. Examples include paying any household bills of an employee, such as telephone, council tax or insurance. However if HMRC has agreed a dispensation for any element of such payments, that dispensation is effective for avoiding a national insurance charge also.

# 14

# Workplace Facilities

## Introduction
Workplace facilities which are necessary for the employment do not create a tax or national insurance liability. There is a specific provision in tax law to ensure that an employee is not taxed on the value of the chair he sits on, nor on heating the workplace.

Where a workplace facility is used other than for the employment, there is generally a tax liability. However, there are exceptions for:
- childcare facilities
- canteen facilities
- sports facilities
- facilities for cyclists.

## Childcare facilities
Generally any childcare provision by an employer is a taxable benefit of the employee, though there are now two exceptions:
- workplace nurseries; and
- childcare vouchers (up to £55 a week).

If the facility comes within the scope of these two exceptions, there is no liable for tax or national insurance. Any childcare facility outside the scope of this exemption must be treated as a taxable benefit.

A workplace nursery is a tax-free benefit only if:
- it takes the form of actual provision of childcare facilities, not payment to an independent facility nor a voucher to be used there
- the provision is offered by the employer, possibly in conjunction with other employers or a local authority or a voluntary body and
- the provisions meet the conditions for childcare set by the local authority.

This tax relief extends to all children of or below school age. It includes looking after children during school holidays and after school.

It is not necessary for the provision to be at the employer's premises or even near the premises. However the employer must be responsible for running the facility.

This tax relief does not cover the employer paying for a nanny or childminder at the employee's home, nor for the use of an independently operated childminding facility.

## Canteen facilities

The use of canteen facilities, including free or subsidised meals, is tax-free provided the facilities are available on equal terms to all employees. If some employees have preferential facilities (commonly known as a golden trough) they are taxed on the cost of providing it. Meals are only tax-free to the extent that they are not excessive.

Free tea and coffee at the work place is not a taxable benefit.

It is not necessary for the employer to run the canteen. If an employer pays someone else to provide canteen facilities, the employees are still entitled to the same tax exemption.

This tax exemption does not apply if the meals are provided elsewhere, such as in a local restaurant, though there are some other provisions which may make them tax-free. For example, an employee is not taxed on hotel meals while away on business.

Another exception is luncheon vouchers. These are tax free up to 15p per working day under a concession unchanged from 1948 (when three shillings would buy a good meal). National insurance is charged on the same basis as for income tax.

## Sports facilities

The use of workplace sports facilities does not create a taxable liability. This covers facilities provided by or for the employer whether or not on the employer's premises. It also includes facilities which several employers have organised together.

This tax exemption does not include:

- membership of a sports club not run by the employer
- facilities not available to all employees
- overnight accommodation
- facilities on domestic premises
- use of yachts, aircraft and cars.

It should be appreciated that some of the above items may be still be tax-free under other provisions, such as when an employee staying away on business uses a hotel swimming pool.

### Facilities for cyclists
There is no tax liable for using certain facilities for employees who cycle to work. Such facilities can include:
- storage for bicycles, cycling clothes and equipment
- changing rooms
- shower facilities
- free breakfast.

# 15

# Relocation

An employer who relocates may offer financial assistance to an employee to help that employee find a new home. The tax laws do not specify how far the employer must move; there is only a general requirement that travelling from the existing home to the new workplace must be unreasonable. Conversely the travelling distance from the new home to the new workplace must be reasonable. There is no statutory definition of 'reasonable', though this seems to have caused no problems in practice. As the law refers to 'travelling distance', travelling time may be of more relevance than distance in miles.

An employer may provide up to £8,000 worth of tax free assistance to an employee. (This figure has remained unchanged since 1993.) The employee does not have to sell his old home to qualify.

This sum may be used to pay for:
- legal fees, estate agent fees, surveyor's fees and similar
- stamp duty land tax
- removal expenses, and temporary storage of furniture
- new carpets, curtains and fitted furniture
- bridging loans
- travel and subsistence while looking for a new home
- the services of a relocation company.

The expenses must be incurred in the tax year of the relocation or in the following tax year. This may be extended if the delay is for reasons beyond the employee's control, such as a child completing examinations or inability to sell the old home.

The sum may not be used to pay for compensation for:
- any loss on the sale of the old home or
- moving to a higher cost housing area.

A relocation company or the employer may agree to buy the employee's old house. The employee will usually avoid any capital gains tax on any profit under the main residence relief. Such an agreement often provides that if the house is sold for an amount above a set figure, all or some of the excess is passed back to the employee.

The exemption for relocation is additional to other exemptions. For example, travel overseas is usually tax-free in its own right. In practice this means that an employee who relocates overseas may receive £8,000 plus travel, while one who relocates in the UK receives £8,000 including travel.

If an employer pays relocation expenses above £8,000, the excess must not be added to gross pay. It is either declared on form P11D resulting in an assessment on the employee, or the tax may be paid by the employer under a PAYE settlement agreement.

The rules for national insurance are completely different. It first depends on whether the employer has a scheme for fixing the amount of relocation payable. If it does, such a payment may be made free of national insurance if::

- this has no element of profit for the employee
- it is based on an accurate survey of the costs involved
- the scheme to fix the payment allows for movements in prices
- the payment is reasonable for the employment involve
-  it is supported by written evidence
- the scheme is considered sound by Inland Revenue.

If the employer has no scheme for fixing relocation expenses, the following may be paid free of national insurance:

- specific additional expenses, such as higher mortgage or rent
- a sum for moving to a higher cost housing area (not allowed for tax), to the extent that the new home is comparable in size and standard to the old one
- payments which are absolutely necessary for the move, such as legal bills and estate agents' fees.

In so far as the relocation expenses meet the relevant conditions, they may be paid without limit, free of national insurance.

The following items of relocation expense are subject to national insurance if paid by the employer:

- any payment towards a general increase in the employee's cost of living
- the cost of moving to a home of a higher standard (such as moving from a semi-detached to a detached house, or one with more bedrooms)

- any expenses which is not absolutely necessary.

If the employer provides an interest-free or low-interest bridging loan, some special provisions apply. Such a loan usually does incur a tax liability, but this tax liability may be postponed.

For example, suppose the other relocation expenses come to £6,000, and the employer grants an interest-free bridging loan of £100,000. The other expenses leave £2,000 of unused exemption from the £8,000 limit. The taxable value of the bridging loan uses the current 'official interest' rate of 5%, giving a benefit value of £5,000. This means that the tax liable is postponed by 2000/5000 of a year, which is 146 days. The tax liable is then calculated on the benefit of £5,000 a year. If the bridging loan is repaid within the 146 days, there is no tax liability.

An employer may wish to provide relocation expenses in excess of what is allowed under the £8,000 exemption. This is permitted, but the employee will incur a tax liability. The employer may settle that tax liability under a PAYE settlement agreement.

For national insurance, the position is:

- the exemption for class 1 national insurance follows that for income tax and
- class 1A national insurance is payable by the employer on qualifying expenses which exceed the £8,000 limit.

# 16

# Other Benefits

## Beneficial loans

A beneficial loan arises when an employee is allowed to borrow money from his employer without paying interest, or by paying a low rate of interest.

Such arrangements are perfectly legal and proper, but can give rise to a tax liability.

It should be noted that the tax liability covers all beneficial loans which arise from the employment, even if the loan is not provided by the employer. Thus a loan provided by an associate company can be a beneficial loan.

It also covers loans to an employee's husband, wife, parent or remoter ancestor, or child or remoter descendant, if the loan arises from the individual's employment, or the husband or wife of an ancestor or descendant. It should be noted that this list of relatives is wider than that used for other taxable benefits. There is no tax charge if the employee can show that he derived no benefit from the loan made to a relative.

The law excludes many types of beneficial loan from a tax liability. Of most relevance, a loan of up to £5,000 is excluded, so there is usually no tax liability on a loan to buy a season ticket.

When a beneficial loan is taxed, the amount of taxable benefit is calculated by applying an 'official rate of interest' to the outstanding loan, from which is deducted any amounts actually paid by the employee. The value of the loan is not added to gross pay, but disclosed on the form P11D at the year-end. The official rate has been 5% since 2002.

There is no tax charge on a beneficial loan if it meets any one of these conditions:

- the amount lent does not exceed £5,000 – if the loan does exceed £5,000, the taxable value is determined on the whole

amount of the loan, not just on the excess
- the employer is a bank or other commercial lender and the loan is a 'commercial loan', that is on the same terms as offered to customers (see below)
- the employer is a relative of the employee and the loan was made in the normal course of the employer's domestic, family or personal relationships
- the loan is to pay inheritance tax or capital transfer tax
- the loan is to buy a life annuity for someone aged 65 or over
- the loan is to purchase plant or machinery for use in a partnership or to acquire an interest in a close company or partnership, or to improve commercially let property.

No tax charge arises on any outstanding loan after an employee's death.

An employee is not taxed on a beneficial loan if it is a commercial loan. That means that its terms are the same as those offered to the employer's customers. As most commercial loans are charged at a rate equivalent to the official rate of interest rate anyway, this provision usually only becomes relevant in protecting an employee from a tax charge when the employer offers low-start mortgages or similar loans.

The value of a beneficial loan is generally calculated by taking the average amount of all loans to the employee outstanding for whole tax months, and multiplying this by the official rate of interest as periodically announced by HMRC.

### Assets lent or given to an employee

When an asset is lent or given to an employee for his personal use, the employee will usually be liable to tax on the value of the asset. If given to the employee, the tax is on the cost to the employer. If lent to the employee, the tax is generally charged on 20% of the asset's value, plus any annual expenditure. So if an employee is provided with television and video equipment costing £1,000, the employee will be taxed each year on £200 worth of benefit.

If the employee makes any contribution towards the use of the asset, this is deducted from the taxable value.

These general provisions do not apply to:
- assets needed for the duties of the employment, such as normal furniture and tools
- assets needed by the employee for security reasons

*89*

- cars, and fuel for cars
- cycling safety equipment
- mobile telephones (up to one per employee)
- shares and other forms of security
- vouchers, or items which may be easily exchanged for cash.

The first five items in this list are not taxable. The other items are taxed under their own rules as explained later.

Before 6 April 2006, there was a separate exemption for computer equipment lent to employees.

There are special provisions when an employer allows an employee to acquire its own goods or services free or at a discount.

Details of assets lent or given to an employee must be disclosed on the form P11D unless, exceptionally, they are the subject of a dispensation. The tax on assets lent or given to an employee may be paid under a PAYE settlement agreement.

The value of an asset is:

- the cost of an asset
- any extra cost in buying the asset
- any extra cost in selecting or testing the asset
- any extra cost of storing or installing the asset; plus
- costs of servicing, maintaining and providing after-sales service.

## Company's own products or services

If an employee is allowed to use or buy the goods or services provided by his employer, this usually creates a taxable benefit on the amount by which any price paid is less than the cost of the goods to the employer. There is no tax charge if the employer allows a discount but still recovers at least the cost of the goods.

The issue of what 'cost' meant in this context was finally resolved by the House of Lords in the leading case Pepper v Hart [1992] STC 898 . This case concerned a private school which allowed a teacher to send his son to the school to fill a vacant place on payment of 20% of the usual fee. This reduced fee was sufficient to cover the marginal cost of one extra boy at the school, such as his stationery, food and laundry. It was not enough to cover the direct cost of one boy, taken as all the school's costs divided by all its pupils, including the teacher's son. The House of Lords, reversing all previous decisions of Inland Revenue (now HMRC) and the lower courts, held that the cost was the marginal cost not the direct cost. As the marginal cost was less than 20% of the usual fee, the teacher did not incur an additional tax liability.

HMRC says that it will regard the following items as not giving rise to any tax liability:

- rail or bus travel by employees provided that no fare-paying passenger is displaced and no extra costs are incurred by the employer
- goods sold at a discount but where the employee has paid at least the wholesale price
- teachers who pay at least 15% of the normal school fees
- professional services which do not require additional employment of partners, and where any direct costs are either negligible or paid by the employee.

## Christmas parties and other social occasions

Entertainment of staff is a taxable benefit to the staff. If it takes the usual form of provision of food, drink and entertainment, there is no national insurance liability. For tax, extra-statutory concession A70 exempts from tax Christmas parties and other social occasions up to £150 per person per year.

This limit applies cumulatively throughout the tax year. Once the limit has been reached, the whole amount of the occasion which breached the limit is taxable. For example, a company has four social occasions per year, each of which costs £60 per head. The first two are within the £150 limit and are tax-free. The third breaches the limit, so the whole £60 is taxable, as is the £60 for the fourth occasion.

The limit is per person attending. Thus the reckoning may include partners, ex-employees and self-employed contractors. It may also include customers and suppliers, but if their number becomes significant, the occasion could be regarded as business entertainment.

Where tax is payable for a Christmas party or other social occasion, the tax will usually be collected under a PAYE settlement agreement.

## Clothing

An employer is generally entitled to make matters of dress and appearance part of the contract of employment, provided the provisions are necessary and reasonable.

Sometimes the employer provides clothing for the employee to wear. This may be protective clothing, a uniform or corporate clothing, or stagewear for those in entertainment.

There are no specific tax provisions on clothing. The rules follow the normal rules for the allowability of expenses. As employees must wear clothing anyway for warmth and decency, the onus is always on the employer or employee to demonstrate that particular clothing meets the conditions for relief.

In practice, there is usually no problem in claiming for:

- protective clothing, such as safety helmets
- specialist clothing, such as diving suits
- uniforms.

Such provision can usually be readily covered by a dispensation.

For some manual jobs, there are fixed allowances agreed with the relevant trade unions. Some of these allowances include clothing costs.

Otherwise, the main conditions for tax relief on clothing are:

- the employee is required to wear such clothing in the employment and
- the clothing is not suitable for normal wear outside the employment.

The former condition is only met if the requirement to wear such clothing is legally enforceable. The enforcement may be from statute (such as under hygiene regulations) or under the contract of employment.

The latter condition was tested in the famous case Mallalieu v Drummond [1983] STC 665 when a lady barrister claimed for skirts and blouses she was required to wear in court and which were too dowdy to wear outside her work. It was held that this these items were not tax-deductible. Although she may not be willing to wear them outside her work, they were of a style which could be worn outside her work. She was allowed to claim for her gown and wig. This case led to a clampdown on what clothing may be claimed.

A difficult area is corporate clothing, which stands halfway between a uniform and normal dress. A company may require its staff to wear smart clothing of a particular colour scheme, perhaps with a company name or logo on. A simple test is whether an ordinary person looking at the employee would realise that the employee was wearing corporate clothing.

If the clothing qualifies for tax relief, so does its laundry. An employee cannot claim for normal clothing even if he can demonstrate that he is required to wear clothing of a specific type, such as an accountant required to wear a pinstripe suit and gold cufflinks. Also, an employee cannot claim for excessive wear. such as a welder suffering extra wear and tear on his normal clothing.

### Medical treatment

Generally, any medical treatment or health insurance paid by the employer is regarded as a taxable benefit to the employee. It is not regarded as an expense of employment as medical treatment can never be 'wholly and exclusively' for the employment but will always be partly for the benefit of the person's normal life. This applies even where there are sound commercial reasons for paying for the treatment, such as paying for private treatment so an employee returns to work sooner, or where an employee's work demands some particularly high standard of sight or hearing.

It is a legal requirement that an employer must offer users of computers free eye tests and, if required, free spectacles. From 6 April 2006 this does not create a tax liability.

There are some exceptions:

- an employee is not liable to tax on medical treatment or insurance when working overseas
- there is no tax charge for medical check-ups which do not involve any treatment.

### Prizes and gifts

An employee may receive prizes or gifts from the employer or from another person in respect of employment. If the gift is received from a third party, such as a present from a supplier, the employee must obtain permission from the employer to keep it. This arises under the law of agency. An employee is the agent of the employer and an agent is not allowed to make a secret profit.

Where a prize or gift is provided as a result of employment, there is generally a tax liability. If the prize or gift takes the form of money, there will usually also be a national insurance liability. However these general rules are subject to many exceptions. It should be appreciated that Inland Revenue treats the employment scope very widely. For example, wedding presents to an employee, prizes for passing examinations and even a present to an employee in hospital are all

*93*

regarded as gifts arising from the employment.

There are special tax provisions for prizes and gifts:
- for staff suggestion schemes
- for long service
- in the form of tips
- for staff social occasions
- from third parties
- between family members.

Where there is a tax liability, the employer may agree to pay the tax under either the Taxed Award Scheme (explained below) or under a PAYE settlement agreement (explained in a separate chapter).

### Staff suggestion scheme

An employee who is rewarded for making a suggestion may be excused tax on it up to a limit.

If the employer takes up the suggestion, the award is only taxed to the extent that it exceeds any one of these limits:
- 50% of the expected net financial benefit in the first year of adoption
- 10% of the expected net financial benefit in the first five years
- £5,000.

For example, an employee is paid £3,000 for a suggestion which is expected to save £12,000 in the first year and £20,000 in the first five years. The three limits above are respectively £6,000, £2,000 and £5,000. The lowest of these is £2,000, so the £1,000 above this figure is taxable.

If the employer does not take up the suggestion, an encouragement award of £25 may be paid tax-free.

### Tips

A tip provided by a third party to an employee, such as a customer tipping a waitress, legally belongs to the employee. At no time does it become the property of the employee.

The case Nerva v R L & G Ltd [1994] established that a tip added to a cheque or credit card payment is also the legal property of the employee, even though the employer must be involved in passing that payment to the employee. A service charge added to the bill in accordance with a notice or menu legally belongs to the employer.

The employee is only entitled to a share of such charge if a contractual entitlement can be established.

If tips are paid for staff generally, such as when there is a dish by the till, the contents must be distributed between staff on an equitable basis. The employer is not entitled to keep any of the tips. Such a collective arrangement is sometimes called a tronc, and the operator of it (usually the employer), the troncmaster.

An employee who is not passed a tip to which he is legally entitled may treat that as an unlawful deduction from wages, and bring a case before the industrial tribunal.

All tips are subject to income tax as they arise from the employment even if not provided by the employer. A tip paid directly by a third party to the employee is not subject to national insurance. However where the employer is involved in paying the tip to the employee, even paying in cash an amount added to a cheque, this is subject to national insurance.

If tips paid centrally are distributed by someone other than the employer, there is generally no national insurance. This arrangement is also known as tronc. It is usually operated by an employee chosen by his or her colleagues, who is known as the troncmaster.

### Long service award

An employee given a present, such as the traditional gold watch, for long service may be excused tax on it.

Such an award is tax-free if:

- it relates to service of at least 20 years
- the value of the item does not exceed £20 per year of service and
- no similar award has been made in the previous ten years.

If the gift does not comply with all these conditions, tax is assessable on the excess.

A long service award made at the end of employment may escape tax if it comes within the scope of a termination payment (see separate chapter).

### Third party gifts

A gift from a third party escapes tax under extra-statutory concession if all these conditions are met:

- the gift consists of goods, or of vouchers which may only be exchanged for goods

- the donor is not the employer or associated with the employer
- the gift is not made in recognition of particular services in the employment, nor in expectation of any particular services
- the gift has not been directly or indirectly procured by the employer
- the total cost of all gifts from the same donor to the same employee do not exceed £250 in any tax year.

For these purposes, a gift made to a member of the employee's family or household is regarded as made to the employee. The value includes VAT, even if the donor is able to reclaim it as input tax.

There is no tax liability if it can be shown that the gift arises from a personal relationship rather than the employer and employee relationship. So if a father employs his son, the son is not liable to tax on a Christmas present from his father.

There are some other limited exceptions, such as:
- certain business entertainment
- presents which have the nature of a personal testimonial to the employee.

Wedding presents are taxable.

### Taxed award scheme

An employer or third party may give an employee a prize, such as a free holiday for being the salesman of the year. Such a prize is a taxable benefit. However the donor may wish to pay the employee's tax so that the impact of the prize is not blunted by a tax bill. An employer may use either the Taxed Award Scheme (TAS) or a PAYE settlement agreement; a third party may only use the Taxed Award Scheme.

The Taxed Award Scheme is a contract between the donor and HMRC. This must be arranged in advance by contacting HMRC

Under the Taxed Award Scheme, the value of the prize must be grossed up by the employee's marginal rate of tax. The donor must:
- pay this tax to Inland Revenue and
- give the employee a certificate showing the amount of the award and the tax paid.

As the tax paid under TAS is a settlement of a personal liability of the employee, it is subject to class 1 national insurance. The national insurance liability cannot be paid under TAS.

For example, an employee is given a holiday costing £3,000. He pays tax at 40%. The cost is grossed up by 66.67% to £5,000 on which the donor pays £2,000 tax. The employer and employee pay class 1 national insurance on that £2,000. In practice this means that the employee will still pay about £200 in additional national insurance.

## Professional subscriptions

An employee may claim against his taxable income for a subscription to a professional body relevant to the employment. The whole subscription may be claimed for any tax year if the employee did relevant work in that tax year, even if the employee was not in relevant employment for the whole year.

HMRC maintains a list of professional bodies whose subscriptions may be claimed. This list is revised annually and published. It may be inspected free on HMRC's website.

If the employer pays the subscription for the employee, it will usually be appropriate for the employer to seek a dispensation. Otherwise the payment must be disclosed on the P11D (see Benefits and Expenses).

An employee cannot generally claim for a subscription to any other body. Thus subscriptions to trade unions and clubs, for example, are not allowable. If the employer pays for such subscriptions, the payment must be disclosed on the P11D form.

The rules are slightly different for national insurance purposes. If the employer pays a subscription, that subscription creates a national insurance liability unless subscription to the body is a condition of the employment. This is a stricter condition than for tax.

## Scholarships

A scholarship awarded by an employer to an employee's child is a taxable benefit which must be disclosed on form P11D and on which the employee is liable to tax.

## Security assets

An employee is not liable to tax on special security assets or services provided to an employee who is exposed to a special risk because of his work. This exemption applies to protection for the employee's family if the employee is also protected.

The special risk must derive from the employment. The examples quoted by Inland Revenue are of security lighting, grilles and alarms for those likely to be targeted by terrorist groups. However the legislation is drawn widely enough to protect gamekeepers from armed poachers, and celebrities from over-zealous fans. Services can include those of bodyguards, security officers and specially trained chauffeurs.

There is no tax relief for normal security equipment, such as personal alarms or security cases, as this is not protecting against a special risk.

To qualify for this exemption from tax:

- the protection must be of people, not property
- the risk must derive from the employment
- the risk must be special to that employment
- equipment must not comprise cars, boats, aircraft or accommodation (though accommodation may qualify under another relief).

There is no tax relief for security equipment or services which the employee provides for himself.

### Telephones

A tax liability for us of a telephone only arises when it is used for personal calls. If so, the liability depends on whether the telephone was a mobile or fixed instrument.

Whether a call is a personal or a business call depends on the purpose of the call, not on its substance or the relationship between the parties. So a call by an employee from his home to find out his duties for the next day is a business call. A call to a supplier to ask a girl there out to dinner is a personal call. Similarly it does not matter if a business call includes some personal conversation such as asking after the person's wellbeing or discussing the weather.

If an employee uses the employer's fixed telephone for a personal call, that is a taxable benefit unless the employee refunds the cost of the call. There is no national insurance liability.

If an employer pays any part of an employee's home telephone bill, this is tax-free to the extent that it only reimburses the employee for the cost of business calls made on his telephone. In practice HMRC will often agree a proportion of the bill.

One mobile telephone may be provided to an employee without incurring any tax liability.

## Training

Training may be regarded as a taxable benefit to the employee, though there are several specific exceptions.

Training provided by the employer is not a taxable benefit, provided that the knowledge is related to the employment or for a possible future employment. This tax relief includes training people to start a new job with the employer.

A possible future employment need not be with the same employer. It includes training for an employee who is leaving to do different work which the employer has agreed to pay as part of a termination package. The conditions are that:

- the employee must have been employed for two years before starting the course or ceasing employment
- the employee must be about to leave or have left within the previous year
- the training must be related to obtaining a new job
- the employee must have left employment no later than two years after the training ends
- the course must not last more than one year
- the training must be in the UK
- the employee must have a good attendance record
- all employees in the same position must have been offered training on similar terms.

This tax exemption covers course fees, examination fees, and necessary books. It also covers travel expenses to the amount that they exceed what the employee's commuting costs were. The tax relief is claimed back if the employee is re-engaged by the employer within two years of the end of the training.

External training paid for by an employer is not a taxable benefit, provided that it relates to the employment or possible future employment.

If the external training lasts at least four continuous weeks, the travelling and subsistence costs may also be paid tax-free. This tax relief is conditional on the training being in the UK, and the employee being paid his normal salary.

If an employer pays for an employee to attend training at a college or university or other place of education, the amounts are tax-free provided:

- the course lasts at least one academic year

- the employee maintains an attendance of at least 20 weeks in the year and
- the amount paid does not exceed £15,000.

## Legal liabilities of employees

There many provisions by which an employee can incur a personal liability in the course of his employment. An employer may meet such a liability without it creating a taxable benefit for the employee.

The liability may be met without creating a tax liability by:

- the employer paying the liability directly
- the employer paying the legal fees to fight the action
- paying premiums to insure against such liability.

An employee who takes out his own insurance may claim tax relief on the premiums.

An insurance policy may protect the employee for up to six years after leaving, and may insure the employee for any liability to the employer.

If the liability is met directly by the employer, tax relief is limited to the risk which could be insured against. Thus, it cannot cover any fine for a criminal act.

## Pensions advice

From 14 December 2004, an employee is not liable to tax on the cost of an employer providing advice about pensions, provided:

- the advice is only about pensions, and not on personal finance generally
- the facility is offered to all employees and
- the cost does not exceed £150 per employee.

## Counselling

Counselling and similar welfare provisions are tax-free provided they relate to helping an employee adjust to the loss of employment or to finding new employment or self-employment.

## Other items

In addition to items mentioned in this and other chapters, there are many special exemptions for particular occupations, such as free coal for miners, helicopter commuting for oilrig workers and word processors for clergy.

Any benefit whose cost to the employer is less than £1 is disregarded.

Despite the many exemptions and provisions, there are many benefits which are taxable though declaring them probably never occurs to either the employer or employee. The following will usually be taxable benefits:

- letting an employee use the photocopier or telephone for personal use
- lending books to an employee to help with an examination
- counselling an employee facing a personal problem such as bereavement or marriage breakdown
- giving flowers or fruit to an employee who is ill
- providing tea and coffee to a partner who is waiting for an employee to finish work.

There have been many attempts to claim for benefits which have been refused. All the following are not exempt from tax:

- meals while working late
- examination fees to qualify for a job
- payments to an agency to find work
- newspapers by journalists looking for stories
- alcoholic drink and beta-blockers by snooker players.

# 17

# Attachment of Earnings Orders

## Types of order

An attachment of earnings order is an instruction to an employer to make regular deductions from an employee's payslip and pay it to a third party. An employer must comply with such an order.

In England and Wales, there are four main types of attachment of earnings order:

(a) attachments of earnings orders made by the courts under the Attachment of Earnings Act 1971 or Courts Act 2003
(b) child support deduction of earnings orders made by the Child Support Agency
(c) community charge or council tax attachments of earnings orders made by local authorities
(d) income support deduction notices made by the Benefits Agency.

The rules for (a) and (b) are almost identical. Orders under (a) may be 'priority' or 'non-priority'.

In Scotland, (a) does not apply. Instead, the courts may order an arrestment of earnings under Debtors (Scotland) Act 1987. This is a different system. Although an arrestment may only be ordered by a Scottish court, it can be applied to an English payroll. Similarly, an English court's attachment of earnings order can be applied to a Scottish payroll.

In Northern Ireland, (c) does not apply as the community charge and council tax have never been levied in Northern Ireland. Orders under (a) are made under separate laws but operate on the same basis.

## Attachments under 1971 Act and child support deduction orders: basics

Attachments of earnings orders (AEOs) made under the 1971 Act and Child Support deduction of earnings orders (CSOs) state:

- an amount to be deducted from each payslip
- the total amount to be collected
- a level of protected earnings.

All new court orders are now made under the 2003 Act. Such orders will gradually replace orders under the 1971 Act. The main difference is that attachments under the 2003 Act are calculated by the employer according to tables, whereas 1971 orders state a fixed amount.

The amounts on AEOs are set by the courts according to their discretion. The figures for CSOs are calculated according to a formula. CSOs have become common since 1996.

For orders under the 1971 Act, the employer must deduct the amount of the attachment as stated unless the deduction would reduce the net pay below the figure for protected earnings. For example, an employee has net pay of £400 a week. The employee receives an AEO which an attachment figure of £120 a week and protected earnings of £300. The full attachment would reduce the net pay to below the protected earnings, so only £100 may be deducted.

If the figures for attachment and protected earnings relate to a period other than that by which the employee is paid, the figures must be adjusted to the pay period. For example, if the AEO mentioned in the previous paragraph was served on an employee who was paid monthly, the figures would be multiplied by 52/12. The attachment would be £520 a month, and protected earnings £1,300. Note that there is a special system for council tax orders where an employee receives payments for different period lengths. This is explained later in this chapter.

The employer must keep a record of the amount deducted against the sum owed. For all but the most complicated and large systems, this can be kept satisfactorily in a notebook. Every time a deduction is made, it is deducted from the sum owed.

In summary, the amount deducted for each order from each payslip is the lowest of:

- the amount of the deduction as calculated in accordance with the order
- the amount which will reduce the employee's net pay to the level of protected earnings
- the balance owing.

*103*

## Priority orders

AEOs issued by the courts under the 1971 Act may be marked 'PRIORITY' in the top right hand corner. These are usually used for unpaid fines and for maintenance payments. Non-priority orders are usually used for civil debts.

The two differences between a priority and non-priority AEO are that:

- a priority order is applied before a non-priority order and
- if the full attachment cannot be made because of the protected earnings, the shortfall is carried forward for priority orders but not for non-priority orders.

## Council tax orders and 2003 Act orders

Council tax orders are issued by a local authority to recover council tax or community charge (imposed before 1993).

Orders may be made by the courts under Courts Act 2003 to recover fines and other payments. There are no priority orders under the 2003 Act. Priority is used to deal with shortfalls; the use of tables related to net earnings ensure that there are no shortfalls.

If community charge or council tax is unpaid, the local authority may obtain an enforcement notice from the magistrates' court. The local authority, not the court, may then issue a CTO without needing to undertake any further legal proceedings.

Unlike AEOs and CSOs, a CTO does not specify the rate at which the amount is to be deducted – it just gives the amount to be collected. The amount to be collected is determined by reference to tables. There is no protected earnings figure for CTOs or 2003 Act orders because the amount is a percentage of earnings, so an element of protection is already provided.

With the order are provided three tables:

- Table A: weekly earnings
- Table B: monthly earnings
- Table C: daily earnings.

The tables give a percentage of the net wages to be attached. Unlike other orders, the employer must:

- calculate the amount of each attachment and
- keep a record to see how much has been paid, stopping when the whole balance has been paid.

The Tables are sent with the order.

## Administration charge

For all types of order, the employer is entitled to deduct £1 for himself every time a payslip is attached. If several orders are deducted from a payslip, the employer may deduct £1 for each one. This administration charge is a contribution to the employer's expenses of operating the system.

The employer is not obliged to make the deduction. It is entirely at the discretion of the employer. It would seem that the employer must deduct either £1 or nothing. The employer cannot, for example, deduct 50p per payslip.

## Earnings defined

For the purposes of all these different types of orders, earnings (or net pay) comprises gross pay less:

* income tax
* employee's national insurance
* contributions to an occupational pension scheme and
* amounts deducted on orders previously applied on the same payslip.

Earnings does not allow for other deductions from income, such as payroll giving, trade union dues or loan repayments. If an employee has a disallowed deduction from gross pay, the attachable earnings will not be a figure which appears on the payslip.

Gross pay includes not only basic pay, but such irregular items as commissions, bonus and overtime payments. Payments of pensions made through a payroll may be attached. It includes holiday pay, and any sick pay or maternity pay provided by the employer if above the statutory amounts (but note that statutory maternity pay cannot be attached).

Attachments may be made from amounts of pension paid from a payroll, except that an attachment cannot reduce a pension below the guaranteed minimum pension (unlikely in practice anyway), or which is paid for disablement or disability.

Gross pay does not include amounts which simply reimburse genuine expenses, but does include allowances which are taxed as income. An attachment is not made when an employer provides an advance on pay, but is made on the next payslip on the amount of net pay including the amount advanced.

The following special categories of earnings also may not be attached:

- sums paid by a public department of the government of Northern Ireland, or of a foreign country
- seamen's wages if the order is for payment of maintenance
- earnings for any service on a fishing boat.

### Sequence of orders

An employee may have more than one form of order outstanding against him at any time. The rules for determining the sequence in which the orders are to be applied depend on whether the orders were received after 31 March 1993.

Assuming that all the orders were issued after 31 March 1993, all current orders may be applied to each payslip, subject to the rules about protected earnings. Each successive order treats as its figure for net pay, the amount after the previous orders have been deducted.

In practice, it is worth noting that CTOs can take years to clear, particularly for low paid employees

All orders are put into one of two categories:

- priority AEOs, child support orders and CTOs
- non-priority AEOs.

All orders in the first category are paid in sequence before those in the second category. Within each category, the orders are paid in the date order they are received.

Each time one order has been applied, the net wage for the next order is the figure after previous orders have been deducted. If you are applying the £1 administration charge, this is made after all attachments have been made.

The employer is required to show on the payslip:

- the amount collected under each order separately; and
- the amount deducted as administration charges.

The employer is not required to provide the employee with a copy of the calculation, nor to explain the calculation, but may do so voluntarily.

### Variations in order

An order may be varied or terminated by the authority that issued it.

The court or Child Support Agent may vary an order at any time. In addition, the magistrates' court may issue a temporary variation order which has the effect of changing the level of protected earnings for up to four weeks.

All variations are effective when received by the employer, except that an employer need not act on a variation within seven days of receiving it.

### Duties of employer

It must be stressed that an employer must comply with these orders. An employer who does not comply can be fined.

The duties of the employer may be summarised as:

(a) to tell the court or Child Support Agency (not a local authority) whether a person is an employee and how much the employee earns – the employer is obliged to provide a written and signed statement on request

(b) (from February 1995) to give the Child Support Agency information necessary to help it establish whether an employee is the parent of a particular child

(c) promptly to advise the issuing authority if an order is received for someone who is not an employee – an employer is also obliged to notify the court on becoming the employer of someone who the employer (unusually) knows has an outstanding AEO

(d) to apply the order when received – except that an order need not be complied with if received less than seven days before the payroll run

(e) to make the deductions correctly in accordance with the order, and to pay the sums deducted to the appropriate authority

(f) to notify the court when the employee leaves employment – the notice must be made within seven days for an AEO or child support order, or 14 days for a council tax/community charge order.

Regarding (a), a local authority does not have the power to require the employer to give details on employees, though there is nothing to stop an employer giving such information voluntarily. Instead, the local authority has power to obtain this information from the employee.

Regarding (e), the period in which the employer must pay over the money deducted will be stated on the order. In practice the period is usually generous – council tax orders typically require payment within 19 days of the end of the month in which the payslips were prepared. If the period given causes problems for the payroll procedure, the employer should write to the appropriate authority, explaining why and asking for a longer period.

Regarding (f), it should be noted that council tax orders are addressed to anyone who has the named person in employment. If the employer knows the name and address of the new employer, the order may be passed to the new employer who may continue applying it without further reference to the local authority. The first employer is still obliged to notify the authority that the employee has left but is not required to give the authority the name and address of the new employer. The authority may obtain this from the employee.

An employer may ask the court to consolidate two or more AEOs. The employer has no authority to question an order, nor to ask for it to be revoked.

The employer is not required to explain or justify an order to the employee, but may do so voluntarily. The employee may go to the court or other authority at any time to seek to have an order varied. For example, if he pays the fine or council tax directly, it is his responsibility to have the order ended. For AEOs, the employee may obtain an explanation of how the system works from court staff.

An employer commits an offence punishable by a fine if he:

- fails to provide information about an employee when properly requested to do so
- fails to inform the authority that the subject of an order is not an employee
- fails to take reasonable steps to comply with an order or variation
- does not notify the authority within the time limit when an employee leaves
- fails to inform the court that he is now the employer of someone he knows has an outstanding AEO (rare in practice)
- gives the court any false information.

The employer is also obliged, in practice, to keep sufficient documentation about the orders as part of the payroll records. Documentation which should be kept comprises:

- the orders themselves
- calculations

- a record of the amount outstanding on each order after each payslip
- the date of leaving, when applicable
- copies of all communications with the authorities, noting the date they were sent or received.

## Council tax orders for payments for different periods

There is a special procedure for council tax orders where, unusually, an employee receives separate payments for different lengths of time which overlap. An example is a salesman who receives his normal salary every month, and receives a separate payment every quarter for his commission.

If the payments are made together, such as an annual bonus simply added to the gross pay on a payslip, this special provision does not apply. The appropriate percentage is applied to the single figure of gross pay.

When this provision does apply, the procedure is that the appropriate Table is only used for the main payment, such as the salesman's basic salary. If it is not clear which payment is the main one, the employer may choose either. The employer must deduct 20% from the other payment.

## Arrestment of earnings

Child support orders and council tax orders apply in Scotland under the same laws as in England and Wales. However instead of AEOs under the 1971 Act, the Scottish courts have a completely different system known as arrestment of earnings.

There are three types of arrestment order:

(a) earnings arrestments
(b) current maintenance arrestments
(c) conjoined arrestment orders.

Of these, (a) is made for unpaid debts, and (b) for unpaid maintenance. Type (c) is made to consolidate orders.

For an earnings arrestment, the court states the amount of the debt. The employer determines the amount to be deducted from tables supplied with the order.

For a current maintenance assessment, the court states the amount to be deducted on a daily basis. The daily rate of pay is calculated by dividing the employee's pay by the number of calendar days since the previous payslip. There is a statutory protected earnings figure of £12 a day. The court may notify a higher protected earnings figure. The deduction is the amount by which the pay exceeds the higher of £12 or the notified amount per day. The latest tables for arrestment of earnings apply from 5 April 2006.

A conjoined arrestment is a combination of the previous two types, each of which is administered under its own rules.

## Income support deduction notices

Income support deduction notices (ISDNs) are issued by the Benefits Agency to recover income support paid to an employee in the 15 days after he returns to work after an industrial dispute. ISDNs are rarely encountered in practice.

The operation of an ISDN is similar to an AEO issued under the 1971 Act. The ISDN specifies an amount to be recovered and a figure for protected weekly earnings. If the employee is not paid weekly, this figure is multiplied by:

- 2 if paid fortnightly
- 4 if paid four-weekly
- 5 if paid monthly.

If the amount of pay exceeds the protected earnings by:

- £1 if paid weekly
- £2 if paid fortnightly
- £4 if paid four-weekly
- £5 if paid monthly,

then 50% of the amount by which net pay exceeds the protected earnings is deducted. Fractions of a penny are always rounded down.

Deductions under an ISDN are made until the earliest of:

- the full amount has been recovered
- the ISDN is 26 weeks old (or older)
- the employment ends for any reason
- the Benefits Agency notifies the employer that the ISDN has been discharged.

The employer may deduct a £1 administrative charge for operating an ISDN.

Payment must be made to the local Benefits Agency office by the 19th of the month following the calendar month in which the deduction was made.

# 18

## Maternity

### Introduction

Maternity covers the periods of pregnancy, childbirth and the period immediately after the birth. In UK law, maternity gives the employee various rights, particularly:

- paid time off work for ante-natal care
- not to be dismissed because of the pregnancy
- the right to return to work after childbirth and
- statutory maternity pay.

These maternity rights may only be claimed by a female employee who becomes pregnant. There are no equivalent paternity rights, nor can maternity rights be claimed by an employee for the adoption of a child. There are however plans to introduce some rights for parental leave in addition to maternity leave.

A woman is usually capable of becoming pregnant from puberty to the menopause, typically from ages 12 to 50. In employment law, there are no age limits for any maternity rights. On average 4% of female employees will become pregnant in any one year, though this is obviously subject to huge variation according to their age profile.

Pregnancy strictly lasts for 38 weeks or nine months. However it is usually counted from the first day of the last menstruation, which usually gives 40 weeks. From this date, an expected date of birth can be determined.

Pregnancy is not an illness or an injury, but a normal function of a female body. However, pregnancy can cause or exacerbate illnesses or injury. In such cases, it is necessary to determine whether the absence is primarily due to sickness or maternity. Legally, an absence is for sickness or maternity, but not both.

Childbirth means the birth of a living baby after at least 24 weeks of pregnancy. A baby who dies during childbirth is regarded as having been born alive.

A stillbirth or abortion operation (where the baby dies or is killed in the womb) is not a childbirth. However many maternity provisions usually relate to the pregnancy rather than the childbirth, so such a woman may still be eligible. The exceptions are statutory maternity pay and maternity restrictions which require childbirth. A woman who is not eligible for the appropriate maternity rights may be eligible for sickness rights instead.

### Restrictions

An employer must carry out a health assessment for all areas where women of child-bearing age work. An employer must not wait until a woman becomes pregnant before attending to the matter. New and expectant mothers must be protected from certain risks, such as lead, radioactivity, heavy loads and certain chemical agents.

A pregnant woman must be protected from exposure to illnesses which are of much less risk to non-pregnant employees. Rubella (German measles) is the commonest such illness. If exposure cannot be avoided, the woman may absent herself from work and claim statutory sick pay.

After childbirth, a woman may not return to work for:

● four weeks, if she works in a factory or
● two weeks otherwise.

### Payment for ante-natal care

An employee is entitled to payment for her absence from work for ante-natal care. A woman cannot be required to make up the hours lost because of an ante-natal visit, nor to rearrange the times of such appointments to minimise disruption at work. She is entitled to her normal pay for her normal hours of work.

In practice, these requirements are usually met simply by ignoring the ante-natal absence and treating the employee as if she was at work.

### Occupational maternity pay

An employer may pay occupational maternity pay (OMP) either voluntarily or under the contract of employment. This is an additional right to statutory maternity pay (SMP), though SMP may count towards the total paid as occupational maternity pay.

Occupational maternity pay is paid according to the agreed conditions, regardless of whether they coincide with the requirements for statutory maternity pay and other maternity rights. For example, OMP may have different notification requirements or be payable at a different rate or for a different period.

## Maternity leave

There are two separate statutory rights to be away from work because of maternity:

- ordinary maternity leave
- additional maternity leave.

Ordinary maternity leave allows a woman to take time off work, regardless of how long she has worked. The time off is 39 weeks from April 2007, 26 weeks previously. It will be extended to 52 weeks by 2012.

During ordinary maternity leave, she is entitled to statutory maternity pay if she has sufficient qualifying service, and maternity allowance if not.

A woman must not return to work until two weeks after the birth. This two-week period is known as compulsory maternity leave. It normally falls within the period of ordinary maternity leave. If, exceptionally, it does not, the period of ordinary maternity leave is extended to the end of compulsory maternity leave.

Additional maternity leave may be taken by a woman who has one year's service by the qualifying week, the 11th week before the expected birth. This runs for 26 weeks from the end of the ordinary maternity leave. A woman receives no pay or statutory maternity pay during this period.

During the period of maternity leave (of all types), the woman remains an employee and is entitled to benefits arising under the contract other than pay. This may include keeping a company car, continuing to accrue holiday entitlement, and contributing to a pension scheme. She is also bound by appropriate conditions of her contract of employment, such as the duty of confidentiality and loyalty.

## Statutory maternity pay

Statutory maternity pay (SMP) is a weekly entitlement payable for up to 18 weeks to an employee who becomes pregnant.

It is payable for six weeks at 90% of average weekly pay, and for the rest of the period at a set rate announced by the government for each tax year. The employer may reclaim a percentage of the statutory maternity pay. The percentage has been 4.5% since 2002.

Statutory maternity pay is regarded as normal pay for all purposes except that attachments of earnings cannot be made from them. Statutory maternity pay is subject to income tax and national insurance in the same way as normal pay.

The set rate is £108.85 a week up to 5 April 2007. The figure usually increases each year in April in line with inflation.

### Eligibility

An employee is eligible for statutory maternity pay if she:

(a) is legally an employee, and not self-employed

(b) earns at least the lower earnings limit for national insurance

(c) is at least 16 years old when the maternity pay period starts – there is no upper age limit

(d) has been continuously employed by the same employer for 26 weeks into the qualifying week (the 15th week before the expected birth) - the broad effect of this is to disqualify someone who was pregnant when she started the employment

(e) is still pregnant in the 11th week before the baby is due

(f) stops working for the employer because of maternity

(g) gives proper notice

(h) provides appropriate medical evidence.

In practice, condition (d) means that a woman is probably entitled to SMP if she became pregnant after starting work for that employer, and is probably not entitled if she was already pregnant when she started. It is irrelevant how many hours a week the employee works.

If an employer decides for any reason, that the employee is not entitled to statutory maternity pay, the employer must provide a letter to this effect. The employee may then be able to claim maternity allowance from the Benefits Agency. Provided a woman earns at least the lower earnings limit for national insurance, the allowance is the set rate for all 18 weeks.

### Definition of terms

The operation of statutory maternity pay uses special terms whose meanings must be clearly understood.

**Expected week of childbirth (EWC)** - is the week, beginning on a Sunday, in which the birth is expected.

**Qualifying week** – is the 15th week before the EWC. An employee must be employed into this week to be eligible for statutory maternity pay.

**Maternity pay period** – is the period for which statutory maternity pay is payable.

**Set rate** – is the fixed weekly amount of statutory maternity pay payable from the seventh week of the maternity pay period.

Because of the problems in accurately determining whether the time-related conditions have been met, Inland Revenue provides tables of dates.

## Notification and evidence

An employee claiming statutory maternity pay must provide both notification and evidence of her pregnancy. The requirements are separate though often dealt with together.

Notification is when the employee informs her employer that she is pregnant. The following points should be noted.

- The employee must give notice herself, though if this is not possible, the employer must accept notification from someone else.
- The employer may insist on written notification (and usually should do so). There is no standard form for this. An employer may design his own form, but must still accept notification in any written form, such as a letter.
- Notification should be given at least 28 days before the maternity pay period starts.

If an employee gives less than 28 days' notice, the employer must decide if there is good reason for the late notification. If the employer accepts that there is good reason, that decision is final. If the employer does not accept the reason, the employee may appeal to the adjudication officer at the local social security office for a ruling.

The period of 28 days is extended to two months from April 2007.

The employee must provide medical evidence to the employer. This evidence must:

- be in writing
- state the week in which the baby is expected
- be signed by a doctor or midwife
- be signed no more than 14 weeks before the expected week of confinement

- be submitted by the third week of the maternity pay period, unless there is good reason for later submission, when evidence may be accepted up to the 13th week.

Evidence is usually given on form MAT B1, but the employer must accept any written evidence, such as a letter, if it meets the conditions above.

Evidence counts as notification provided it is made early enough.

## Maternity pay period

The maternity pay period is the period for which statutory maternity pay is payable. Note that statutory maternity pay is currently payable only for whole weeks starting on a Sunday, though this changes in April 2007.

The employee chooses when her maternity pay period (MPP) starts, subject to these rules.

- The MPP always starts on a Sunday;
- The MPP must start no earlier than the 11th week before the expected week of confinement, and no later than the Sunday on or after the actual birth. If, exceptionally, the baby is born before the 11th week before the EWC, the MPP starts from the Sunday on or after the birth;
- The MPP starts automatically if she suffers a pregnancy-related illness in the six weeks before the EWC.

If a woman does any work for her employer during the MPP, she loses SMP for the whole of that week. An exception of 'keeping in touch days' is introduced from April 2007. These allow a woman to come back for a few odd days before returning full time.

## Sickness

If a woman is suffers from a pregnancy-related illness in the six weeks before the expected week of confinement but before the date she has chosen to start her maternity pay period, the maternity pay period automatically starts, and her choice of starting date is ignored.

If she is suffering from such an illness when she reaches the sixth week before the EWC, her maternity pay period starts six weeks before the EWC.

If she suffers from a pregnancy-related illness during this six-week period, the maternity pay period starts from the Sunday on or after the start of the illness.

Note that this provision about pregnancy-related illness is triggered by the illness, not the absence. If a woman is sick at a weekend in the six weeks before the EWC, the employer must determine whether the sickness started before Sunday.

If she suffers from an illness which is not pregnancy-related, she is paid statutory sick pay (provided she meets its other conditions) up to the start of the maternity pay period, and statutory maternity pay thereafter. Note that statutory maternity pay and statutory sick pay cannot be paid in the same week.

The employer must decide whether an illness or injury is pregnancy-related. The Benefits Agency has produced guidance in notice NI200. If there is doubt, the employer should seek further information from the employee, and possibly medical advice.

The maternity pay period ends on the earliest of:

- 26 or (from April 2007) 39 weeks after its start
- when the employee starts working for another employer, which the employee is required to notify her employer paying SMP
- when she is imprisoned or
- her death.

Note that the maternity pay period always ends on a Saturday. If any of the above fall on another day of the week, the maternity pay period ends on the following Saturday.

## Amount of statutory maternity pay

Statutory maternity pay is paid at two rates:

- 90% of average wages for the first six weeks; and
- a set rate for the remaining weeks.

Average earnings is basically all remuneration subject to class 1 national insurance, averaged over the eight weeks before the qualifying week. This is explained in more detail below.

If 90% of average earnings is below the set rate, the set rate is paid for the first six weeks.

The set rate is a fixed weekly amount announced by the government for each tax year. Since 1994 it has been the same amount as for statutory sick pay. The rate is £108.85 in 2006/07, and usually increases each year from April in line with inflation. You use the rate in force when the payment is made.

## Calculation of average earnings

Earnings, for this purpose, is broadly anything subject to class 1 national insurance. It thus includes all salary, wages, bonuses, commission, statutory sick pay and overtime. It does not include benefits which are not subject to national insurance, such as a company car or beneficial loan. Earnings are not reduced by pension contributions, as these are not deducted from gross pay in calculating national insurance. xxx

For a *weekly-paid employee*, the average is calculated by taking the payslips paid in the eight weeks before the end of the qualifying week, and dividing the total by 8.

For a *monthly-paid employee*, the average is:

• the amount on the last pay day before the qualifying week plus all other payments made in the previous eight weeks
• divided by the nearest number of whole months to which those payments relate (usually 2, occasionally 3) and
• multiplied by 12 and divided by 52.

This is basically the average weekly pay over a two-month period.

If an employee is paid at intervals other than weekly or monthly, the procedure is to:

• add the last payslip before the qualifying week to all those paid in the previous eight weeks
• if this represents a whole number of weeks, to divide by that number of weeks. If not, to divide by the number of calendar days represented and multiply by 7.

Fractions of a penny are always rounded up to the next whole penny.

Note that, with one exception, the average earnings is always based on the amount paid in the period, regardless of to what it relates. Thus if an annual bonus or backpay falls within the period, that is included. (The one exception refers to backpay paid after the period but which relates to it, and is explained below under 'Gillespie ruling').

This rule applies even if the employer and employee agree to manipulate the date of an annual bonus or commission so that it falls in this period to boost the amount paid for the first six weeks.

Directors are entitled to statutory maternity pay on the same basis as other employees, but with a special provision for voted fees.

If an employee receives backpay after the period used to calculate the average earnings, but which relates to earnings in that period, the average weekly pay must be adjusted. This is known as the Gillespie ruling after the case brought before the European Court of Justice and decided on 13 February 1996.

## Payment of statutory maternity pay

Normally statutory maternity pay is paid at the same time and at the same intervals as her normal pay. So if she was paid monthly by cheque, that is how she may be paid her statutory maternity pay.

However the regulations allow the employer to choose whatever method is convenient. For example, if she was paid weekly in cash, her statutory maternity pay could be paid by cheque.

## Recovery from the state

An employer may recover a percentage of statutory maternity pay from the state.

The recovery rate is either:

- 92% or
- 100% plus a compensation payment.

The compensation payment is a further percentage announced for each tax year. It is 4.5% for 2006/07. This compensation payment reflects the fact that the employer has paid employer's national insurance on the statutory maternity pay.

An employer uses the higher recovery rate only if he is a 'small employer'. This means that the employer paid £45,000 or less in national insurance in the previous tax year. This figure comprises employer's and employees' national insurance, less recovery of statutory maternity pay and statutory sick pay.

Where an employer did not employ people for the whole of the previous tax year, eligibility for the higher rate of recovery is determined according to the national insurance paid in the current year. This is determined by adding up the national insurance payable in the year so far, dividing this by the number of tax months which have elapsed, and multiplying by 12.

The recoverable amount of statutory maternity pay is deducted from the national insurance payable for that month. If this is insufficient, the excess may be deducted from the tax payable. If, exceptionally, that is also insufficient, the excess will be refunded directly to the employer on application.

## Special circumstances

**Multiple employment** – a woman with two or more employments may claim statutory maternity pay from each of them if she meets all the conditions for each of them. She is entitled to ask for two or more copies of form MAT B1.

**Early birth** – normally a birth before the expected date makes no difference to statutory maternity pay.

If a woman gives birth before the qualifying week and, but for the early birth, she would have 26 weeks' continuous employment into the qualifying week she meets the continuous employment condition for statutory maternity pay. Also, the period for which average earnings are determined use the last pay date before the actual birth instead of the last pay date before the qualifying week.

If she gives birth before the maternity pay period has started, the maternity pay period starts from the Sunday on or immediately after the birth.

If she gives birth before she has been able to give 21 days' notice of pregnancy, she must give notice within 21 days after the birth, unless this is not possible, when it must be given as soon as possible.

**Late birth** – a late birth does not affect statutory maternity pay in any way, even if the maternity pay period has ended.

**Stillbirth** – a stillbirth is when the baby is dead before birth. If the baby lives for an instant out of the womb, it is regarded as a live birth.

Statutory maternity pay is payable in respect of a stillbirth if the pregnancy lasted at least until 16 weeks before the expected week of confinement. If it did not, she may be entitled to statutory sick pay instead.

**Multiple birth** – statutory maternity pay is not affected by the woman having twins or any other multiple birth. Statutory maternity pay relates to the pregnancy not to the babies.

## Resignation or dismissal

A woman may not be dismissed for being pregnant, but she may be dismissed for another reason if it constitutes fair dismissal. Pregnancy does not provide an immunity from the normal laws on dismissal.

A woman who resigns or is dismissed after the start of the qualifying week remains entitled to statutory maternity pay.

## Industrial action

Any week in which a woman took part in industrial action is excluded in determining whether the 26 weeks' continuous employment condition has been met, even if she only took action for part of the week.

## Sickness and injury

Periods of absence for sickness or injury are regarded as part of the continuous employment, provided she was kept on the payroll.

Sickness up to the start of the maternity pay period does not affect the entitlement to statutory maternity pay, unless it is pregnancy-related illness in the six weeks before the expected week of childbirth.

## Disputed decision

If an employee successfully appeals against an employer's decision not to pay statutory maternity pay, the employer must either pay the statutory maternity pay within the time limit set by the adjudication officer, or appeal against the decision. If the appeal is refused, the employer must pay the statutory maternity pay as soon as possible after the refusal.

## Payment beyond the maternity pay period

If an employer pays statutory maternity pay beyond the maternity pay period, he may not recover any of the payment from the state. In fact, such payments are not regarded as statutory maternity pay at all.

If the extra payment arose from a mistake, the employer may be able to recover it from the employee under the rules explained in the chapter on Errors. If the extra payment was deliberate, it is regarded as additional pay.

## Record keeping

The only statutory maternity pay form which an employee must use is SMP 1, which must be completed and handed to a woman who claims statutory maternity pay which the employer refuses for any reason.

The method for recording statutory maternity pay is whatever method is most convenient for the payroll system. The records must be sufficient to identify:

- the amounts of statutory maternity pay paid to each employee
- when the statutory maternity pay was paid and

- the total amount of statutory maternity pay paid in the tax year.

Other forms are provided for an employer who may wish to use them. In practice, all such information is now held on computer.

The PAYE payment records must also record the amount of statutory maternity pay recovered from each payment, and how this has been calculated.

The amounts of statutory maternity pay paid for each employee are disclosed on the year-end returns.

## Adoption

From 6 April 2003, statutory adoption pay (SAP) is available to a man or woman who adopts a child. Many of the rules are the same as for SMP. One significant difference is that the employee must have worked for that employer for 26 weeks before the adoption, not 26 weeks into a qualifying week. (There is no qualifying week for adoption pay.)

The employer must see a 'matching certificate' which confirms that the adoption has been approved. SAP may only be claimed for new adoptions, so it cannot be claimed (for example) when someone marries a natural parent and adopts the child, nor when a foster carer adopts a foster child.

Adoption leave is granted and SAP is paid on the same broad basis and at the same rate as for SMP.

If a couple adopts a child, only one matching certificate is issued and the couple must decide which of them claims these adoption rights. The other partner may claim paternity leave and statutory paternity pay (even if female).

## Paternity

Since 6 April 2003, fathers are allowed two weeks' paternity leave and statutory paternity pay (SPP). This right is also given to the partner of a person claiming adoption leave and SAP, even if that person is female. The leaves may only be taken as whole weeks, not as odd days. Paternity leave must be completed no later than 56 days after the birth or adoption.

The father must have worked for 26 weeks into the qualifying week (15 weeks before expected birth) to qualify. It is not necessary for the father to be married to the mother or even to be the child's biological father; the requirement is that the man is the woman's partner and accepts responsibility for the child.

SPP is paid at the same rate as SMP.

From April 2007, a woman who does not use all her entitlement to maternity leave may transfer the unused leave to the father to extend his paternity leave.

# 19

## Statutory Sick Pay

### Overview

Statutory sick pay (SSP) is a daily entitlement payable for up to 28 weeks to an employee who is absent from work for sickness. It is payable from the fourth calendar day of sickness.

It is payable at a fixed weekly rate which the government revises annually. The employer may be able to reclaim some of the statutory sick pay from the state.

Statutory sick pay is regarded as normal pay for all payroll purposes. It is subject to tax and national insurance. Attachments of earnings orders may be made from SSP.

### Opt-out

An employer may decide not to operate statutory sick pay at all. This is conditional on the employer providing occupational sick pay or normal pay of at least the same amount and on the same conditions as for statutory sick pay.

The employee must not in any week be worse off than if he was receiving statutory sick pay. An employer may not, for example, stop occupational sick pay after 20 weeks, or impose tougher notification requirements or exclude sporting injuries. An employee remains eligible to claim his rights under the statutory sick pay even if the employer has opted out. For example, the employee may still require a form SSP 1(L) and may still refer any refusal to pay sick pay to a social security adjudication officer.

The following points should be noted about opting out of statutory sick pay.

- There is no formal registration or authorisation. An employer may opt out and back in at will.
- An employer may opt out for some employees and not others.
- Basic records of when sickness started and what was paid and

when must still be kept and made available to social security inspectors.

- An opted-out employer may still make a claim of statutory sick pay from the state if the conditions for the percentage threshold scheme are met.

## Eligibility

An employee is eligible for statutory sick pay if he or she:

- is legally an employee, and not self-employed
- earns at least the lower earnings limit for national insurance
- is contracted to work or has worked for at least three months
- has done some work under the contract of employment.

It is irrelevant how many hours the employee works or (generally) how long he has been employed.

Statutory sick pay is not paid:

- to an employee in legal custody
- to a woman during her maternity pay period
- during an industrial dispute in which the employee is involved
- to a foreign-going mariner.

An employee can also be ineligible for SSP if he has recently been paid certain social security benefits, or if he has had a recent period of sickness which, with the current absence, exceeds 28 weeks.

## Definition of terms

The payment of statutory sick pay uses special terms whose meanings must be clearly understood.

**Qualifying day** – a day on which an employee is entitled to statutory sick pay.

**Period of incapacity for work (PIW)** – period for which an employee may be entitled to statutory sick pay.

**Waiting days** – the first three days of a period of sickness for which an employee is not entitled to statutory sick pay.

**Linked PIW** – two PIWs which are treated as one because they are separated by 56 or fewer days.

## Sickness

Statutory sick pay is payable for periods of:

- sickness (as defined below)

- precautionary reasons (such as to stop a pregnant woman catching rubella)
- convalescence certified as necessary by a medical practitioner
- periods for which the employee is certified as a carrier of an infectious disease.

Statutory sick pay is not payable for periods of:
- compassionate leave, such as to look after a sick child
- routine visits to the doctor, dentist, optician etc
- absence for cosmetic surgery
- sabbaticals, or resting other than necessary convalescence.

Sickness is defined as 'a specific disease or bodily or mental disablement of doing work which he or she can reasonably be expected to do under the contract'.

The following points should be noted about this definition.
- The disease or disablement must be specific. Statutory sick pay is not payable for being generally run down, for example.
- An employee must be prevented from doing any work under his contract of employment. For example a shop assistant with a broken leg whose job involves some driving is not sick if he is capable of still working in the shop.
- An employee is sick even if he is capable of doing a different job. For example, a driver recovering from a broken leg cannot be required to do office work until his leg heals.

For statutory sick pay, it does not matter how the person came by the illness or injury. An employee who is injured while decorating his house or playing football remains eligible for statutory sick pay.

### Notification and evidence
An employee must provide both notification and evidence of sickness. The employer has some freedom as to what notification and evidence is required, subject to some limits.

For notification, an employer may generally state how and when an employee must notify absence, subject to certain limits. In particular, the employer must:
- make any rules known to all employees
- say by which day of absence (usually the first) notification must be received, but cannot insist on a time of day

- accept notification sent by post as being made on the day it was posted
- not require the notification to come from only the employee
- not insist on evidence as the only form of acceptable notification
- not refuse any written notification sufficient to show that the employee was sick
- allow later notification when it is not reasonably possible for the employee to have made earlier notification.

An employer may make less onerous notification conditions for a second absence arising from the same cause.

If the employer has not made any such rules, the employee has seven days in which to notify the employer.

For evidence, the following points should be noted.

- An employer must accept a medical certificate signed by a doctor, unless, exceptionally, the employer has evidence to suspect its validity.
- An employer has discretion on whether to accept a medical certificate signed by someone other than a doctor, such as an osteopath, chiropractor, herbalist or acupuncturist.
- An employer may ask for a self-certificate of sickness for any period of sickness, but is not required to do so.
- An employer may ask for a doctor's certificate for any period of sickness which has exceeded seven days, but is not required to do so. An employer cannot insist on a doctor's certificate for fewer than seven days' absence.
- An employer is not obliged to refund any charge a doctor may make to an employee for issuing a medical certificate.

## Occupational sick pay

An employer may pay occupational sick pay under the contract of employment. Such payments are subject to whatever rules are agreed in the contract.

In particular, the rules may say that occupational sick pay is not payable for certain absences, such as sporting injuries. The rules for occupational sick pay may also have stricter rules for notification and evidence.

Amounts of occupational sick pay may count towards the statutory sick pay entitlement, but not so that an employee loses any entitlement he has under SSP rules. For example, an employer may pay full salary for any sickness up to 13 weeks. The employer would then be required to pay statutory sick pay for any sickness for the next 15 weeks.

## Doubt about sickness

An employer has no right to demand that an employee be examined by a company doctor, unless the contract of employment specifically includes such a provision. An employee may agree to independent examination, but cannot be compelled to do so.

An employer must in the first instance decide whether the employee is sick. If the employer is satisfied, that decision is final. If not, the employer may refuse to pay statutory sick pay. The employee then has the right to appeal to a social security adjudication officer. There is no such right of appeal if statutory sick pay is refused for non-compliance with the rules of notification or evidence.

If an employee has been absent for sickness for more than four periods of between four and seven days in any 12-month period, and the employer doubts that these absences were for sickness, the employer may ask the Department of Social Security to help investigate the matter.

## Period of incapacity for work

Statutory sick pay is payable for a period of incapacity for work (PIW), up to 28 weeks.

A PIW starts from the fourth calendar day of any sickness. As this includes non-working days, the employer can be required to ask an employee when a sickness started. For a Monday-to-Friday employee, the PIW will start on Thursday if the sickness started on Monday, but on Tuesday if the sickness started on Saturday. The first three days of sickness are called waiting days.

If a PIW starts within 57 days of the end of a previous PIW, the two periods are said to be a linked PIW. It is irrelevant whether the latter absence was for the same cause as the former. This means that the two absences are treated as one absence. The two consequences of this are:

- there are generally no waiting days for the latter absence; statutory sick pay is payable from the first day of sickness and
- both absences are counted to see if the 28-week limit has been reached.

There is an exception in that if the former PIW was served in another employment, there are three waiting days for the latter absence.

There is no PIW for an absence of three or fewer days, even if it falls within 56 days of a previous PIW.

Note that PIWs can cover any number of absences separated by fewer than 57 days, and can last indefinitely.

Inland Revenue produces tables of dates to make it easy to see if two dates are more than 56 days apart.

### Sufficient earnings

An employee is only entitled to statutory sick pay if his average weekly earnings are above the lower earnings limit for national insurance (£84 for 2006/07). Other than to see if this condition is met, the amount of an employee's pay is irrelevant for statutory sick pay purposes.

In many cases it will be obvious that the earnings are above the threshold and no calculation will be necessary. In marginal cases, the average is generally taken over the previous eight weeks' pay slips. For monthly paid staff, the average is the last two months' payslips multiplied by 6/52.

If the employee has not yet worked eight weeks, the average is taken of the payslips issued so far, counting any payment for part of a week as for so many sevenths of a week. If the employee has not received any payslips, the average is the contracted amount of weekly pay. If the employee has done no work at all, he is not entitled to statutory sick pay.

### Amount of statutory sick pay

Statutory sick pay is paid at a daily rate, unlike statutory maternity pay. The amount is announced annually by the government for each tax year.

The amount is expressed as a weekly figure. For 2006/07, this is £70.05. For PIWs of less than a whole week, this figure must be converted to a daily rate. The daily rate is the weekly figure divided by the number of days which the employee normally works.

### Payment

Statutory sick pay is usually paid in the same manner as normal pay. However, the employer may use any reasonable method but must pay the statutory sick pay in cash.

Deductions may be made from statutory sick pay as for other pay, but statutory sick pay may only be offset against liabilities of the same day. This is particularly relevant for retail deductions. A deduction cannot be made from statutory sick pay unless the loss arose on the day that the employee went sick.

End of statutory sick pay

The liability to statutory sick pay ends on the earliest of:

- the employee returning to work
- the employee leaving that employment
- the death of the employee
- the employee going into legal custody
- the 28th week of a period of incapacity for work (including a linked PIW)
- the start of a woman's maternity pay period
- the end of a linked period of incapacity for work of three years with the same employer.

The last of these conditions may seem unnecessary when SSP stops after 28 weeks. However it can arise when SSP has not been paid earlier in a period of incapacity for work because the employee is ineligible for another reason.

## Recovery from the state

An employer of any size may recover any amount of statutory sick pay which exceeds 13% of the national insurance payable for the same tax month. The figure for national insurance comprises employer's national insurance and employees' national insurance before any recovery of statutory maternity pay or statutory sick pay.

For example, a company has paid £400 in national insurance and £162 in statutory sick pay one month. Its may recover:

| | |
|---|---|
| statutory sick pay paid: | £162.00 |
| less 13% of national insurance | £52.00 |
| SSP recoverable | £110.00 |

If an employer has separate PAYE-registered payrolls, the national insurance figure is the total for all payrolls.

Any recovery of statutory sick pay is deducted from the national insurance payable for that month. If that is insufficient, the excess may be deducted from the income tax payable.

The PAYE records must contain sufficient details to identify when statutory sick pay has been recovered from PAYE payments. The regulations do not prescribe any particular method. Whatever method is used, details of the calculation must be kept as part of the payroll records and be available for inspection by Contributions Agency officers.

## Forms

The only forms which an employer must now keep are SSP1 and SSP1(L).

Form SSP1 is given to an employee who is sick but does not qualify for statutory sick pay. It may help the employee to claim sickness benefit from the social security office. An employer may design his own version of this form.

Form SSP1(L) is a leaver's statement for an employee who had a period of incapacity for work which ended in the eight weeks before leaving. This form is only provided to an employee who asks for it.

Amounts of statutory sick pay are shown on the year-end PAYE return, and on the P14/P60 forms.

Inland Revenue also provides a form SSP2 which an employer may use to record statutory sick pay. The use of this form is voluntary.

## Records

Statutory sick pay records are part of the payroll records of the business. They must be sufficient to show for each employee:

- all sickness lasting for more than four days
- any days of a PIW for which statutory sick pay was not paid, and the reason why
- the qualifying days in each PIW
- any leaver's statement received when the employee started
- any leaver's statement provided when the employee left.

It is also advisable to keep:

- all notifications received (including notes of telephoned notifications if the employer accepts these)
- all doctor's and other certificates accepted as evidence
- details of rules about notification and evidence
- details of any applications to and decisions from the adjudication officer.

*131*

# 20

## Pensions

### Introduction
Pension administration is a specialist area outside normal payroll work. However payroll administrators should have an understanding of pensions as it can affect several areas of payroll, particularly national insurance and contribution calculations.

It is also possible for pensions to be paid through a special payroll. Pensions enjoy considerable tax advantages. In particular:
* pension contributions are tax-deductible
* any lump sum payable on death is tax-free.

Pension funds also tend to grow at a higher rate than many other investments. During the 20th century they maintained an average growth of 6.5%.

Because of the preferential tax rules, there are strict rules governing all types of pension scheme.

### Sources of pension
In broad terms, the funding for a pension comes from one of three sources:
* the state
* the employer
* the individual.

### State pension
The state pension comprises a basic retirement pension payable from retirement age to all those who have a sufficient national insurance record. Those who do not, receive a smaller state pension from the age of 80.

In addition, an employee may gain additional pension. Between 1961 and 1975 this was graduated pension in which units were bought according to earnings. Anyone who worked between these years will have acquired units which, from retirement, generate a weekly pension at a value reviewed each tax year.

From 6 April 1978, additional pension takes the form of the State Earnings-Related Pension Scheme (SERPS). Any employee who earns at least the lower earnings limit for national insurance and who is not contracted out is automatically a member of SERPS. An employee may be contracted out of SERPS by being a member of an approved occupational pension scheme run by the employer. From 1 July 1988, it has also been possible for an employee to contract himself out by an appropriate personal pension scheme (APPS).

## Employer pension scheme

An employer may set up a pension scheme to which employees may belong. No employer is obliged to set up a scheme and no employee can be compelled to join.

If the scheme is approved, the employee:

- receives tax relief on the contributions paid and any additional voluntary contributions (provided a generous statutory limit is not breached) and
- pays a lower 'contracted-out' rate of national insurance.

The gross pay is reduced by the amount of contributions for the purposes of income tax, but not for national insurance.

A contracted-out company scheme may either be:

- final salary (also known as 'defined benefit' or 'salary related') (COSRS) or
- money purchase (COMPS).

In COSRS, the amount of pension is related to the employee's final salary. In COMPS, the amount of pension is whatever the contributions relating to that employee will buy as an annuity.

For a scheme to be approved, it must meet various conditions, including these maximum benefits:

- pension of up to two-thirds final salary (after 20 years) on retirement between ages 50 and 70 (with different rules for those who joined before 1989)
- a lump sum on retirement of up to 1½ times final salary. This is tax-free, and reduces the amount of regular pension payable
- a widow's benefits of two-thirds the pension which would have been payable to the employee (i.e. four-ninths of final salary)

- death-in-service benefit of up to four times salary.

There are many conditions to the above maxima, and many other conditions which apply to all forms of pension fund. The exact terms of a pension scheme will be found in its trust deed.

### Private pension scheme
From 1 July 1988, an individual, employed or self-employed, has been able to take out an appropriate personal pension scheme (APPS). Contributions to the scheme are tax-deductible up to generous limits depending on age. Private pension schemes are money purchase schemes.

### Contracted-out national insurance
Because part of the national insurance contributions go towards providing the SERPS pension, those who are not in SERPS do not pay so much national insurance. Employees in a contracted-out occupational pension scheme run by the employer pay a lower contracted-out rate of national insurance.

The rebate is given by reducing the rates of employer's national insurance and employees' national insurance between the lower earnings limit and upper earnings limit by so many percentage points. The number of points depends on whether the scheme is a contracted out salary related scheme or contracted out money purchase scheme.

Employees who are contracted out by a personal pension scheme (an APPS) pay the full amount of national insurance. It is not reduced by the reductions above. Instead the DSS pays into the pension scheme an amount equal to the reductions.

### Age related rebates
From 6 April 1997 there is a further complication in that age-related rebates are introduced. These rebates are introduced to address the fact that younger employees have longer for their contributions to gain in value. The employee pays the same amount of national insurance (including the same rebates for contracted out schemes) regardless of age.

### Pensionable earnings
The amount of tax relief depends on 'pensionable earnings'. This is not always the same as the employee's gross pay.

In law, pensionable earnings may include anything subject employment income tax. Thus it may include overtime, bonuses and all taxable fringe benefits, such as the value of a company car.

The actual pensionable earnings are as defined by the trust deed. This is likely to say that pensionable earnings are:

- basic pay only, with no allowance for overtime, bonuses or benefits in kind;
- the gross pay as at a certain date, such as 1 January each year. This means that pensionable earnings are not immediately increased if the pay is increased later in the year.

## Stakeholder pensions

From April 2001, an employer with five or more employees must offer them the option of the new stakeholder pension. An employee who is already a member of an occupational pension scheme may have a stakeholder pension as well, provided he does not earn more than £30,000 a year.

A person may contribute up to £3,600 a year into a stakeholder pension regardless of income. If the limits for personal pension contributions gives a higher figure, a person may contribute up to that higher figure into a stakeholder pension.

In addition to the generous contribution limit, a stakeholder pension is limited to charging no more than 1% of payments as expenses.

Contributions to a stakeholder pension are made net of tax, which is recovered by the scheme.

# 21

# Directors

## Introduction

Directors of companies are treated as employees and must have their earnings subject to PAYE and national insurance in a way similar to employees. There are some special provisions for directors, particularly for national insurance purposes.

A partner or sole proprietor is not treated as an employee of his business, even if a payroll is run for that business.

Directors' remuneration is often dealt with a separate payroll on the grounds of confidentiality.

## PAYE

PAYE for a director is triggered on an amount on the earliest of:

- when the payment is actually made
- when the director becomes entitled to the payment
- when the payment is credited in the company accounts, even if the director cannot draw the money straightway or the account is not in the director's name and
- when the remuneration is determined.

Of these four dates, only the first two apply to employees other than directors.

## National insurance

A director often has the ability to time his payments so that his year's emoluments could be paid in one week. This would mean that the director would avoid much national insurance. To deal with this, there are two special provisions for directors.

The first is simply that advances are treated as pay for national insurance purposes, which is not the case for other employees. When the director is paid the balance less the advance, national insurance is only payable on the balance.

The second is that a director always has an earnings period of the tax year, not a tax week or tax month. The exception is when an employee becomes a director during the tax year. His earnings period starts from his appointment to the end of the tax year. However the whole tax year is usually the earnings period when a person ceases to be a director regardless of when the cessation was in it.

There are broadly two methods to calculate a director's national insurance:

- the total earnings method and
- the average earnings method.

Under the total earnings method, a director and his employer pays no national insurance until the cumulative earnings in the tax period have reached the annual lower earnings limit. This applies even if the director is paid monthly and the first monthly payment exceeds the monthly limit. Once the cumulative earnings have reached the annual lower earnings limit, national insurance is payable on the excess until the annual upper earnings limit when no further employee's national insurance is payable, though employer's national insurance is still payable. This means that the director will pay no or little national insurance early in the tax year, but a higher amount later in the tax year.

Under the average earnings method, the cumulative pay may have national insurance calculated as if the cumulative pay represents a proportion of the annual income. This method may only be used if the employer and director agree. The procedure is:

- calculate the cumulative annual income
- calculate the monthly equivalent
- determine the employee's and employer's national insurance national insurance for that monthly equivalent
- multiply these national insurance figures by the number of tax months so far
- subtract from the total, the national insurance payable thus far.

The last steps are similar to the way PAYE is operated for a normal cumulative tax code.

It will be seen that the annual equivalent ends up the same as the actual cumulative total. There is no advantage to employer or director in using this method, other than the possible convenience to the director of having his national insurance spread evenly. If all his monthly payments are above the upper earnings limit, even this token advantage disappears. There is a cashflow disadvantage in that some national insurance is paid earlier than if the annual earnings method is used.

### Dividends

Directors often withdraw funds as dividends rather than salary, because of the preferential tax treatment, particularly the complete avoidance of national insurance. Since 7 December 1993, a dividend which is legal under company law cannot be taxed as earnings.

### Statutory maternity pay

A director may receive statutory maternity pay. If the director is paid contractually, the average earnings are calculated according to the normal earnings period, in the same way as for any other employee. If the director is paid a sum voted by shareholders, the average weekly pay must be calculated by using the basis for calculating monthly pay to a weekly average.

### Miscellaneous provisions

The following points should also be noted about directors and pay.

- A director of a company is usually a P11D employee (for taxation of expenses), even if earnings are below £8,500 a year.
- Directors can be made personally liable for losses of the company in some circumstances, usually when the director has been fraudulent or negligent. A director is not usually liable for any unpaid PAYE or national insurance.
- There is a specific offence of paying a director without tax being deducted.
- Someone is not entitled to be paid just because he or she is a director. The right must come from the articles of association, shareholders' agreement or contract of employment.
- Amounts of directors' remuneration must be disclosed in company accounts.

# Index

National minimum wage, 16
*Nerva v R L & G Ltd,* 94
Net pay, 25
Notice, payment in lieu of, 52
Notification (SMP), 113
  (SSP), 124
NT code, 33
Number of payrolls, 8
Number plates, 64
Nurseries, 83
Nurseries, workplace, 58

Occupational maternity pay, 110
Occupational pensions, 133
Occupational sick pay, 127
Optical discs, 11
Ordinary maternity leave, 113
OT code, 33
Output work, 18
Overpayments, 23
Overseas service, final pay, 51
Overseas, national insurance, 42
  personal expenses, 73

P codes, 33
P11D expenses, 59
P45 certificate, death, 55
  issue, 50
  joining, 44
  not produced, 46
  payments after, 51
P46 certificate, 46
Paid leave, 21
Parental leave, 22
Parties, 91
Partnership shares, 26
Paternity, 122
Pay after leaving, 51
Pay As You Earn, 29
Pay day, 13
Pay reference period, 17
PAYE settlement agreements, 34
PAYE, 29
Payment in lieu of notice, 52
Payment methods, 9

Payment periods, NI, 40
Payroll giving, 27
Payroll method, 11
  runs, 29
Pension contributions, 30
Pensionable earnings, 134
Pensioner, on payroll, 51
Pensions advice, 100
Pensions, 132
Pensions, NI, 36
Period of incapacity for work, 125
Personal incidental expenses, 73
  records, 14
  representative, 54
Petrol, 66
*Pook v Owen,* 69
Precautionary sick leave, 126
Preferential share purchase, 76
Pregnancy, 111
Pregnancy-related illness, 116
Premature birth, 122
Primary contributions, 35
Priority attachment orders, 102
Private pension schemes, 134
Prizes, 93
Professional subscriptions, 97
Profit-sharing, 77
Protective clothing, 92
Public holidays, 22

Qualifying day, 125
Qualifying week, 115
Quarter 4, 32
Quarterly payments, 31

Rateable value, 80
Record-keeping, 10
Reduced rate NI, 36
Redundancy, 53
Registering with HMRC, 14
Relocation expenses, 85
Resignation, SMP, 120
Restaurant service charge, 94
Retail trade deductions, 26
Retention of records, 10

Waiting days, 125
Week 52 etc, 32
Week's pay defined, 4
Women, NI, 36
  retirement age, 38
Working from home, 71
Workplace facilities, 82
Workplace nurseries, 58
Works bus, 59
Wrongful dismissal payment, 52

X code, 39

Y code, 39
Year-end routines, 32
Young workers, NMW, 17